6/15

D1708784

DATE DUE

HO **SI** NG
BA

Sartor

nd Poultry

4880 Lower Valley Road • Atglen, PA 19310

Originally published © 2010 HEEL
Verlag GmbH under the title,
Selbst Rauchern: Fleisch, Fisch und
Geflugel.
Translated by Omicron Language
Solutions, LLC.

Photograph Credits:
Photocuisine, Potsdam: pages 6, 8-9,
10, 29, 37, 38-39, 50, 60-61, 75, 78-79,
82-83
Stockfood Munich: pages 14, 15, 16, 17,
27, 31, 32, 47, 48 bottom, 52, 55, 58, 62,
78, 96, 103, 104, 108
Fotolia: pages 27, 34, 35, 40, 42, 44,
46, 48 top, 62, 66, 73, 82-83, 84-85,
93, 94-95, 114-115, 128
Pixelio: pages 19, 21, 43, 123
Simone Riefke: page 24
Ramon Wink, WINK PHOTOGRAPHER
GmbH: page 20
Beelonia GmbH: pages 22-23
Cover: Photocuisine, Potsdam, Inset:
Fotolia

Library of Congress Control Number: 2014931021

ISBN: 978-0-7643-4653-8
Printed in China

Published by Schiffer Publishing, Ltd.
4880 Lower Valley Road
Atglen, PA 19310
Phone: (610) 593-1777; Fax: (610) 593-2002
E-mail: Info@schifferbooks.com

For our complete selection of fine books on this and related subjects,
please visit our website at www.schifferbooks.com. You may also write
for a free catalog.

This book may be purchased from the publisher. Please try your book-
store first.

We are always looking for people to write books on new and related
subjects. If you have an idea for a book, please contact us at proposals@
schifferbooks.com.

Schiffer Publishing's titles are available at special discounts for bulk
purchases for sales promotions or premiums. Special editions, including personalized covers, corporate imprints, and excerpts can be created
in large quantities for special needs. For more information, contact the
publisher.

HOME
SMOKING
BASICS For Meat, Fish, and Poultry

Contents

Preface

Smoking food has a millennial-old tradition; yet, during all that time, the process itself has not changed. Today, however, we no longer smoke food to preserve it, but rather to enrich it and make it taste better. What was once a way to preserve food has now become a method to prepare "delicacies." Smoking food also has a nostalgic quality: it has something that, in our highly technological world, takes us back to our roots.

It wasn't that long ago when I served some guests something I had smoked myself for the first time. I served them duck breast on lentil salad. Quite frankly, it was a kind of a test meal. At the time, I was working in the office of a well-known women's magazine and we had just begun a series about different methods of cooking. The idea of "smoking in a wok" had especially piqued me; I really wanted to try it out and share the results with my friends. As I could see in the test kitchen, it was a simple matter and the results were really delicious. The evening was certainly a great success and my friends were not only impressed, they wanted to know just how to do it.

Later, while cleaning the kitchen, I remembered my school holidays, which I sometimes spent with my grandparents. There was a fish farm near where they lived, and the fish farmer smoked his trout, carp, pike and char in a specially built brick smoker in his back yard. I have never forgotten the smell of smoldering beech and juniper wood, which surrounded his land. I must have been nine or ten years old when my grandfather took a fresh salmon he had been given by a friend, to his neighbor to pickle and then hang up in the smoker. A few days later, the two of us ate a few slices of fresh smoked fish. This was the first time I ever ate such a delicacy! The very tender fish, with its wonderful aroma, served on thin slices of toast with a little sour cream, was something extraordinary for me, something that only adults would be able to enjoy. My grandfather was happy to see how good it tasted to me. That day, I received, so to speak, my culinary ordination.

While I was sitting in my kitchen and thinking about my childhood, I got the idea to make a real smoker. Of course you can always buy excellent quality smoked salmon, but, like everything else, anything you smoke yourself simply has a whole other taste dimension. In the meantime, I have smoked a lot of salmon and other fish, as well as poultry and meat; in the beginning, not always with the desired success, but the results kept getting better over time. Don't be discouraged: smoking food is a matter of experience, and this book should help, step by step, give you confidence in preparing food using this special method.

Maria Sartor

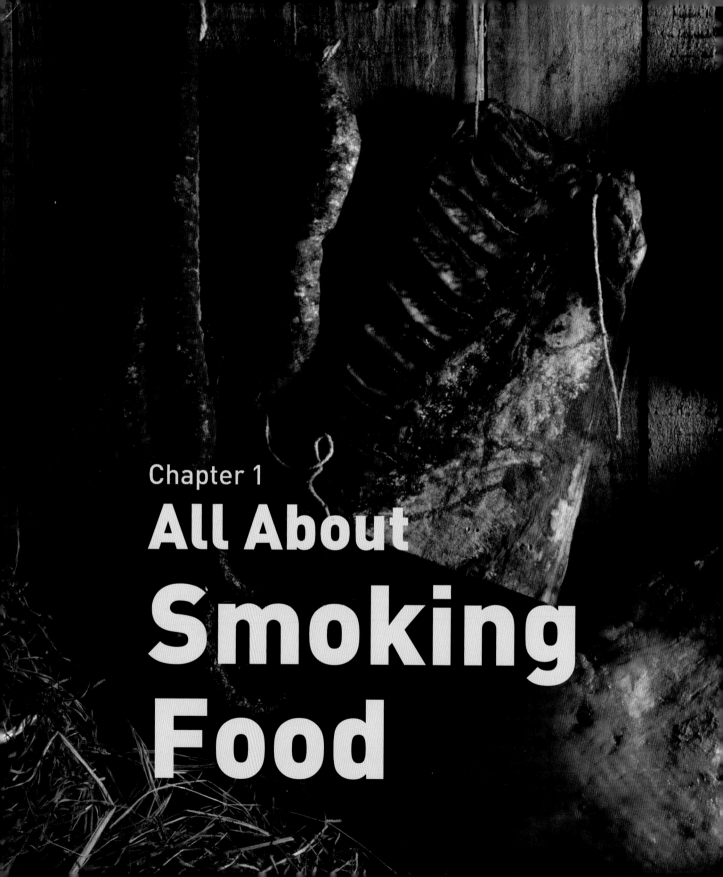

Chapter 1
All About Smoking Food

A Short History of Smoked Food

Since all the huge mammals, such as mammoths, giant deer and steppe bison, became extinct at the end of the last great Ice Age, living conditions changed dramatically for people during the Neolithic period. Earlier, they had moved with their families, following the big herds of animals to secure their food by hunting; now, people became settled, and began to domesticate goats and sheep and to breed livestock wherever they were. Previously, people had collected fruits and grains; now, they grew plants and grain near their dwellings. The change in the climate brought changing seasons, and with it the challenge of storing supplies for the winter.

There is no documentation of when primitive man began to preserve foods, but it is well accepted that salting, smoking, and drying were the first preservation techniques men used. The preferred type of preservation used depended on the local climatic conditions. In dry areas such as southern Europe, Africa, and the Near East, it was easy to dry pieces of meat and fish by hanging them in the storeroom. In northern Europe and in the humid regions on the coasts, smoking was preferred: people simply hung up the food in the house smoke vent. As archaeological evidence shows, this method has been in use for over 9,000 years.

As people neither could explain why food would spoil, nor knew why foods were preserved under certain conditions, they made the gods responsible. Smoke especially was thought to banish evil spirits. As is written in the Bible: "The evil spirits fly before smoke" (Tobit 8, verse 3). And, as we know from the Christmas story, frankincense and myrrh for smoking were precious gifts.

Down till the present day, smoke has been used to cleanse and purify in all the religions of the world, including the Christian. Think of what is known as the "Rauhnächte" (also "Rauchnächte" or "Nights of Smoke") in Austria — the days between Christmas and January 6 — when, in the countryside in Austria, southern Germany and Switzerland, the demons which had made mischief in the past year, are literally "smoked out" from the farm houses and barns by the village priest.

In the following millennia, mankind developed other ways to preserve food, such as pickling fish and meat in oil, or vegetables and fruits in vinegar, alcohol or honey. Thus, it was in China — and not in Europe — that sauerkraut was invented: first, they salted cabbage (also other vegetables).

The liquid created then fermented, with help of the lactic acid bacteria from the air; this made lactic acid, which helped preserve the food. Beyond that, the pickled cabbage was not only especially tasty, but was also healthy and lasted through the winter.

In the history of food storage, methods used to preserve meat and fish played a large part, not only because these foods are very important for the diet, but they also spoil the fastest. Salting was one such method, which was already in use by 2500 BC in Babylonia. Yet it still took about two and a half thousand years until people in ancient Rome discovered that, under certain circumstances, the salts used would color the meat red. The sea salt, with this coloring effect, was harvested on the Mediterranean coast; the salt contains bacteria-killing nitrite, which stabilizes the pigments in the muscles (see page 30).

However, it was the Dutchman de Beukels who first described in the fourteenth century how adding nitrate salts to cooking salt would both improve the preservation of the meat and at the same time conserve its appetizing color. For this reason, de Beukels is considered the inventor of curing or pickling, which is where the process got its name. People then began to take cured or pickled fish and meat and smoke it, improving the keeping quality as well as the taste. In addition, you could always get some smoked food from the storeroom and enjoy it right away. If the food was dried or just salted, you had to first cook it for a long time, or soak it, before you could eat it. No wonder that smoking became the most popular method of preserving food for centuries, especially north of the Alps.

Up into the nineteenth century, there were no alternatives to the traditional methods of preservation. It was not until the French confectioner Appert invented the process of canning food, and, fifty years later, until Louis Pasteur developed pasteurization — killing bacteria by briefly heating the food to 140-195°F (60-90°C) — that food storage could be revolutionized. It has only been since refrigeration made its way into private households in the 1960s that preservation finally became dispensable.

Smoking food, however, became a matter of taste; it is considered a way to make meat and fish even better. Smoked foods are now regarded as a delicacy and smoking food yourself is more popular than ever.

A Brief Overview of the History of Food Preservation

(from Stäudel and Wöhrmann, 1997, Geschichte der Lebensmittelkonservierung [History of Preserving Food])

Prehistoric times and the Stone Age	Salting, smoking, drying
9,000 BC	Use of preservative qualities of milk, honey, vegetable juices
3000 BC	Preservation with oil (Mesopotamia)
circa 2000 BC	Pickling in vinegar (Egypt)
circa 1000 BC	Gas storage: storing grains with formation of carbon dioxide
24-79 AD	Pliny reported how fruits were preserved by coating them (with clay or wax), and on preservative properties of various acids
circa 200 AD	Evaporative cooling (Roman Empire)
circa 1000 AD	Pickling in alcohol (Arabia), preserving with lactic acid (East Asia, the Orient), preserving with sugar (East Asia, the Orient)
1353	Preserving with sugar (Europe)
1397	Brining, possibly already by 2500 BC (Babylonia) and 400 AD (Roman Empire)
1647–1714	Denis Papin created the first "canning" of meat. He heated and preserved meat in his airtight and sealed "Papin cooking pot." However, it remained a laboratory experiment.
1809	Nicolas Appert invented the "tin can," i.e., food is put into airtight containers and heated in a water bath for a certain time
1864	Louis Pasteur developed pasteurization, the brief heating of food to 140-195°F (60-90°C) to kill microorganisms
1937	Preservation by freezing at 0°F (-18°C). However, most households only got access to this since the early 1960s.

What Happens When You Smoke Food?

During the process of smoking, fish or meat are exposed to heat and smoke for a certain period of time. In earlier times, this was done primarily to increase its keeping quality, because the effect of the smoke would gradually decrease moisture in the food, and kill putrefying bacteria. Today, we smoke food mostly because we want to make it especially delicious and give it an appetizing color.

The smoke is produced by the smoldering or incomplete combustion — in the specialized terminology of chemistry — of sawdust, wood shavings, or logs.

As the wood smolders, over 300 different substances form in the smoke. The main ones are:

• **Phenols** have an antibacterial effect and prevent fat oxidation, thereby preventing meat and fish from becoming rancid.

• **Formaldehyde** prevents the growth of yeasts and molds. It also creates a cross-linking of proteins in the tissues, which also releases water at the same time. This causes the leather-like skin of the meat.

• **Carboxylic acids (formic, acetic, carboxylic acid esters)** are responsible for the well-appreciated smoked flavor.

• **Polycyclic aromatic hydrocarbons, such as benzopyrene** are carcinogenic substances, which are filtered out in modern smokers or the smoking is done outside their range. There are legal regulations on the benzopyrene content of smoked foods. Beyond these gaseous substances, smoke also contains ash, soot, tar, and resins, which cling to the outer skin of the smoked food.

Smoking Methods

Because of the differences in climate conditions, people in different continents, or even just regions of the world, developed their own specific ways to smoke foods. Humidity near the coastal areas and the cooler climate in mountainous regions would create different results from the smoking process. Now, we distinguish among cold, warm, and hot smoking — the food is smoked at different temperatures, and that means, for different lengths of time.

The smoking process itself is also divided into two steps: the actual smoking and a period of time when the food is exposed to fresh air. To smoke the food, the "smoke," as the fuel that makes the smoke is called, is heaped up in the smoker's pan or fire chamber, and lighted. When the fuel begins to smolder and smoke develops, it starts the process of smoking the food. More fuel is heaped on the fire several times, as the food gets smoked.

So-called "hallway" or "lean-to" smoking is one of the original European ways of smoking food, and is occasionally still used today as it was a thousand years ago. In a large room, passageway, or entryway, smoke is made by an open fire or smoldering sawdust on the hearth. The room temperature is not artificially controlled; it results from the outside air coming through an open window or skylight, and this is determined by the seasonal weather patterns. This smoking process may take several months to complete.

The method used to smoke the food, basically, depends on what you want for the product: Hot or warm smoking is used for something you will consume soon, while cold-smoked products will last a long time and can be kept in the storeroom. Cold smoked fish or meat will keep for at least fourteen days; hot smoked, for four to six days. Vacuum-packed, the smoked food will even keep for up to six weeks.

Chapter 1

Cottage Smoking

A once very popular way of smoking was the so-called Katenräuchern or "cottage smoking" (a "Kate" is a small cottage). Cottage smoking is done using burning peat and moss, and creates an especially sooty coating on the food but also an intense smoke flavor much appreciated by connoisseurs. However, there are many cancer-causing substances in this smoke and, for this reason, the amateur smoker should not try cottage smoking. There is no problem with eating purchased products, such as cottage-smoked ham and hard sausages, since these harmful substances are eliminated during the processing.

Hot Smoking

Hot smoking is a process in which raw meat or fish is usually cooked between 150-390°F (65-200°C) for a certain period. Essentially, the higher the temperature, the shorter the smoking time. The smoked food is brined and then dried beforehand.

Hot smoked food tastes best if you enjoy it immediately; it generally will keep for a few days. This is the most popular type of smoking, not only among anglers and campers, but also in town, either on the balcony or in the backyard.

Hot Smoked Fish

The washed and scaled fish is brined in a mild solution for about an hour, rinsed off, and dried for several hours. The fish is then cooked in hot smoke in the smoker at a temperature between 150-250°F (65-120°C). How long the fish must be smoked depends on the type and size of the fish; the timing is between 30 minutes and 2 hours. Trout, salmon, and eel are the most popular fish among smoking fans. (See recipes on pages 40 and 62.)

Hot Smoked Meat

The same rules apply for smoking pieces of meat or poultry parts as for fish: First, the pieces are brined, dried, and then smoked. Only with larger pieces of meat, such as a ham, might it might be advisable to boil it before smoking, to ensure it cooks through. How long to smoke the meat also depends on the size of the meat pieces. (See recipes on pages 50 and 75.)

Warm Smoking

Warm smoking is done at temperatures of 85-140°F (30-60°C). Depending on what you are smoking, the process can take anywhere from two hours to twenty-four hours, during which the relative humidity should be kept at 50-85%. Do not extinguish the smoldering fire during the smoking process; this means that there are no periods of just fresh air, as is done when cold smoking.

In warm smoking, no cooking process takes place; the smoked food is still raw and is considered especially tender and juicy, which is very much appreciated by connoisseurs. Warm smoked meat or fish keeps for slightly longer than hot smoked. Warm smoking is the most used process in the food industry, and typical warm smoked products include pre-cooked sausages and smoked pork loin.

Cold Smoking
Cold smoking is a days- or weeks-long process, because the smoking temperature is maintained at between just 60 and 85°F (15 and 30°C). However, cold-smoked foods also keeps the longest. For the most part, ham and sausages are smoked either in a smoker, which has to be of a specific height, or in a smokehouse, which either has its own special stove or has smoke passed through it from the house chimney. As a result, there is usually no continuous smoking process. It is just this intermittent exposure to fresh air that is very important for this kind of smoking process.

Cold Smoked Fish

Fish is wonderful for cold smoking. Just as for meat, you brine and dry the fish before putting it in the smoker. Anyone who loves smoked salmon knows just how delicious cold-smoked fish tastes. However, since preservation for lengthy periods is no longer the primary issue for private households, today fish is usually hot smoked. We generally buy cold smoked fish already prepared.

Cold Smoked Meat

Ham and sausages are cold smoked primarily to make them keep longer. You can also cold smoke game and poultry, such as wild boar or turkey breast. This process takes much longer and is more complex than hot or warm smoking. The meat is cured or brined, a process that takes several days, sometimes even weeks (see page 30), and then the brine is thoroughly rinsed off and the meat hung out to dry in the air. Only then is it smoked. If you have no real smokehouse, you can also do cold smoking in a smaller smoker, in which the meat is hung, at 60°F (15°C) to maximum 75°F (25°C) for two to six weeks.

There are also different phases to this smoking process, alternating from smoking to hanging the food in the fresh air. First, bring the fuel to make the smoke to a smolder when it starts to release smoke. When the wood chips you had heaped on the fire die out — usually after a few hours — the next phase is fresh air, and outside air is let into the smoker. The smoking fuel is re-stocked and heaped up again repeatedly during the overall process of smoking the food. (Depending on whether you are smoking meat, ham, or sausage, 3-5 times.

Smoking with Liquid Smoke

When wood burns (at temperatures up to 1220°F/660°C), it generates smoke that condenses during cooling; this is then collected and unwanted by-products, such as tar and ash, are removed. We call this fluid, which looks like a brown, viscous oil, "liquid smoke."

In the food industry, liquid smoke is being increasingly used as a more hygienic and convenient alternative to wood shavings or sawdust: The meat is put in a temperature-controlled chamber and sprayed with liquid smoke. Depending on the product, it is hot- or cold-smoked. Note: It is not yet legal for private individuals to smoke food this way.

Opinions differ on whether ham made with real smoke or liquid smoke tastes better. The product packaging must state the technique used in its preparation: If smoked over wood chips, "smoke" is listed among the ingredients; if liquid smoke is used instead, it is "smoke flavor."

Different Woods –
and Other Ways to Flavor the Smoke

Which wood you want to use for smoking is primarily a matter of taste, but you must always use a so-called hardwood — a wood that contains little resin. Resins create heavy soot that not only significantly affects the taste, but also is harmful to a person's health. For example, fir or pine wood, even if it smells just as aromatic, is not suitable for smoking food.

The most popular wood for smoking comes from beech trees. Also good are other low-resin woods, such as oak, maple, chestnut, alder, poplar, acacia, willow, or fruit woods (cherry, plum, apple, or pear). Every wood lends its own special flavor to the smoked food; therefore, it is recommended to start out using tasteless beech wood and only then to experiment with other types of wood. Whatever kind of wood you use, the logs must be free of bark, which gives the smoked food a bitter taste. Beyond this, the wood must be dry enough to burn. Some residual moisture is sometimes an advantage, because it promotes the development of smoke. What is very important is that the logs must be natural and can in no circumstances have been chemically treated.

Special Woods

To give the smoke an even more seasoned touch, you can add chips of hickory, mesquite, orange tree, walnut tree, vine, or cedar wood and sawdust from these woods to the smoking wood you have chosen. In addition to a beautiful color, they give a special flavor to fish and meat.

The following recommendations are only a rough guideline. If you feel like experimenting, you will find out very quickly what type of wood, or what combination of wood, you like best.

Tip:

To generate as much smoke as possible, spray any added special wood, herbs, or spices briefly with some water before you lay them on the wood chips or sawdust.

Beech is the universal wood and can be used for all everything.
Alder is the wood of choice for shellfish or fish.
Fruit tree wood (cherry, apple, plum) is particularly good for oily fish, such as salmon, herring, and mackerel, as well as for pork and poultry.
Walnut wood is wonderful with pork.
Vine wood is recommended for game, duck, and beef while
Olive wood lends crustaceans and shellfish a very special taste and is also suitable for cheese.

And this creates even more flavor

You can achieve even finer flavor nuances if you add to the wood chips or sawdust dried herbs, such as rosemary, thyme, or sage, while cinnamon sticks, dried lemon or orange peel, nut shells, black tea, bay leaves, and juniper berries create an especially well-seasoned smoke. Don't set any limits on your imagination if you enjoy trying out new things.

Chipped or Ground Wood

Whether you use logs, chips, or sawdust depends on the size of your smoker: for example, if you are using a larger smoker, you can use logs, which should be only half the size used for firewood. If you are using a tabletop smoker, of course, sawdust is the best choice. Basically, the bigger the pieces of wood, the harder it is to regulate the fire.

As already noted, beech chips are very popular because of the neutral flavor. You can also buy chips of oak or alder. The best would be to start with one of these woods, and gradually add other chips, until you find the composition that best suits your taste. Take notes so you can repeat successful results; while experimenting, smoke only one or two pieces of fish or meat at a time so that you don't have to throw away everything if something goes wrong. You should only buy wood sawdust or chips for smoking in specialty stores, such as fishing shops and well-stocked hardware stores, or from specialized vendors' on the Internet, because they sell just wood for smoking that is free of impurities. It is better not to get sawdust or chips from a cabinetmaker's or woodworker's shop. There, the sawdust often comes from chipwood or plywood treated with synthetic binders, which produces smoke harmful to the health. This also goes for sawdust and chips of painted or treated wood, such as from waste construction timber, fence posts, or boat remains.

You should never use peat, turf, or moss for smoking because, when they smolder, these fuels generate soot, which is harmful to your health.

Equipment for Smoking

There are very simple pieces of equipment with which you can smoke food very well — if you can deal with them properly. Instead of the wood fire used earlier, today people rely on other sources of heat, such as gas or electricity, or you can use an alcohol-fueled smoker, which can be used everywhere, such as in the backyard or for camping (see also "Home-built Equipment," page 24).

For use at home, smaller smokers are sufficient; these come in different sizes for 2 to 12 portions of fish. They all follow the same principle: the sawdust, possibly with added flavorings, is put on the bottom of the smoker and then the prepared food is placed on the grate over the drip tray and the smoker closed with a cover or hatch. The heat source at the bottom of the smoker is then turned on or lit. The heat starts the sawdust smoldering, which creates the hot smoke to cook the fish or meat.

Smoking in an Electric Smoker

It is very easy to smoke food using an electrical hot smoker. For four portions, you only need a tabletop unit. The temperature is regulated by a thermostat and the cooking time is set on a timer. Use sawdust to make the smoke and then scatter dried herbs or spices on it in the pan. Turn on the unit and, when the sawdust smolders, slide in the dripping pan and then the oiled grill with the meat or fish to be smoked. Now, close the door and only reopen it when the timer goes off. The advantages of this kind of smoker are obvious: It requires only a socket and you don't have to provide fuel. There is also no need to monitor the smoking temperature; it is always accurate and the smoked food comes out perfectly cooked.

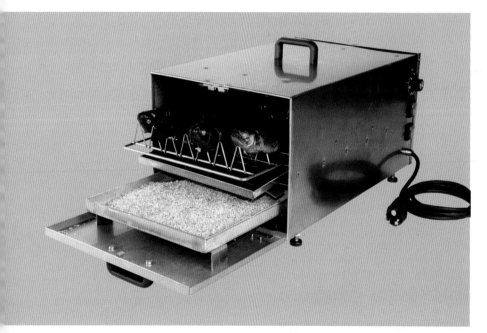

Smoking in an Alcohol Stove

Alcohol units are an inexpensive alternative to electric smokers. They consist of an alcohol burner, sawdust pan, cover, grill, and the case. The sawdust is scattered into the pan and heated. When it smolders, add spices or herbs on top, put in the drip tray, and then lay the food to be smoked on the oiled grill, which you insert over the pan. Now, put on the cover. The temperature inside the smoker can reach 212°F (100°C), so be careful when you open the lid after the smoking time is over.

Smoking with "Professional" Equipment

However, if you are planning not to just smoke food as a hobby, but as a serious enterprise, perhaps even for a livelihood, you have to acquire a professional smokehouse or smoker. Good electric smokers made from steel are available.

How to Build Your Own Barrel Smoker

If you have handyman or craftsman skills, then you might enjoy building your own smoker. This is quite simple:

You will need:
• 1 small metal garbage can, capacity about 13 gallons (50 liters)
• Welding wire, 1/16″ to 1/8″ (2-3mm) diameter
• 6 bricks
• Aluminum foil
• A clean tin can

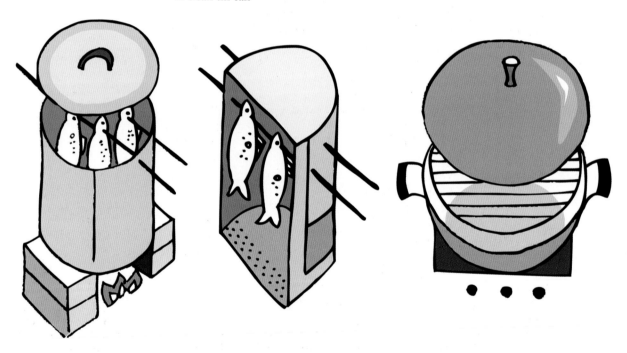

Garbage cans frequently have an internal coating of an insulating layer of lacquer, which can't be immediately detected. For safety reasons, before you use your smoker the first time, you should first light a fire inside, until it reaches a high temperature. Take care when you buy it that the can seams are grooved or welded, and if possible not soldered, since those could easily melt.

On each side, drill two small holes in the metal next to each other and opposite those on the facing side. These should be at least 1" (3cm) below the upper edge so that when the food to be smoked is hung inside, the cover closes tightly and firmly. Take care that the holes you drill are no larger than the diameter of the welding wire, which will later pass through them, so no smoke can escape from the barrel smoker. The distance between the holes must be wide enough so that the fish or meat pieces do not touch each other during the smoking. It is best to position the wires exactly on top of the barrel beforehand, just where you want to install them, and then mark about 1" (3cm), where you will drill the holes, on the outside of the barrel.

Smoking in Your Home-Built Smoker
Pull the wires out of the holes. Spread 5-6 tablespoons of smoking sawdust on the bottom of the barrel. To make sure that no fat from the meat or fish will drip onto the smoldering sawdust, cover the sawdust with a piece of aluminum foil, which has to be slightly larger than the diameter of the barrel bottom. It catches the dripping fat and thus prevents any harmful substances from developing in the smoke. To prevent the fat running over the edge into the embers, fold up the foil and press it against the inner side of the barrel. Plenty of smoke will still find its way up into the barrel.

Make three columns of the bricks, two bricks each, and position them in a U-shape. In the middle, put the tin can, half-filled with alcohol. Light the alcohol with a long match and set the prepared smoker barrel on the bricks. As soon as there is enough smoke, hang the pieces of meat or fish on hooks, which you can buy any fisherman's store, or put it on spit rods, and then hang the rods in the smoking barrel (see also page 26). (Spit rods are metal skewers — similar to shish kebab skewers — pointed at one end and the other end is bent into a hoop. You can buy them in fishing or sporting shops or make them from wire yourself. "Spit rod" is a term used by anglers.) Pay attention when you hang the pieces of meat or fish side by side, that they don't touch each other, and don't come into contact with the aluminum foil or the barrel sides. Both become very hot during smoking, and will burn the food.

Once you have hung the food to be smoked in the barrel, press the lid on firmly, so that no smoke can escape. You could also lay a wet cloth over the barrel before putting on the cover.

As long as the burner is going under the barrel, keep the lid closed, so no smoke or heat escape. Handle it only if the smoking time is over. When the smoking time is over, extinguish the alcohol burner and carefully open the cover. Once the smoke has is gone, take out the smoked food and let it cool for a while, before you serve it lukewarm. When your smoker has cooled off, clean it. Shake the burnt sawdust out of the barrel and rinse the hooks under hot water. Clean the wires which hold the hooks, and your barrel smoker is already ready to use again.

TIP:

Stores for household goods or camping equipment sell fuel cans containing ethanol gel. They are also used to heat fondue pots and are easy to use.

Chapter 1

The Right Way to Hang Your Food

If not put on properly, fish can easily fall off the hooks, so always be careful to hang them up the right way. You can suspend the fish using different kinds of smoking, from spit rods and on cords that you loop around the fishtails.

Worm hooks can be used for eels and small fish up to seven ounces (200g).

Double hooks work better for trout and pieces of fish.

S-hooks are the most typical kinds of hooks and can be used for any piece of fish and meat. All hooks should be made of stainless steel or aluminum.

Many hobby smokers make spit rods of stainless wire themselves: stick the wire through the fish just below the head and next to the spine. The advantage is that, depending on the size of the smoker, you can smoke several fish on one wire. The fish should not be touching (see photo).

Smoking in a Roasting Pan

You can get wonderful results smoking smaller amounts of food in your kitchen by using a roasting pan — best a cast iron one — or a large soup pot with a rack. If you do not have a grill or rack, you can buy one in a kitchenware or hardware store; they come in various sizes. For smoking, proceed using the instructions given for the home-made barrel smoker: spread the sawdust to make the smoke on the bottom, cover with aluminum foil, set the grill or rack holding the food to be smoked on top of the foil, replace the lid, and set the roaster over the heat source.

Smoking in a Wok

The simplest smoking technique for beginners is to smoke your food in a wok. First, put a large piece of aluminum foil in the wok, sprinkle in 2-3 tablespoons of sawdust to make the smoke, and add herbs or spices of your choice. Now, lay another piece of aluminum foil on top and close the wok with the cover. Heat the sawdust over a stove burner on medium heat. Lightly oil the grill rack and lay the food, such as a duck breast, on it (see recipe on page 57). Once the sawdust becomes fragrant, put the rack into the wok and immediately replace the lid. On page 57, you can read how long you have to smoke a duck breast.

Smoking in the BBQ or Grill

A kettle grill is also ideal for smoking. Lay a few short, thin pieces of wood, such as alder and beech, on the bottom of the barbecue and light it. Open the air vents under the grill to make sure it burns well. Once the fire is going and the wood is just smoldering, use the tongs to push it to one side and sprinkle moistened special wood chips, such as hickory, walnut, or vine wood, on top. Now, set a foil pan in the empty place next to the embers, to collect the dripping fat. Brush the part of the grill above the pan with oil and set it over the embers. Add the food and close the grill lid. You can read how long it will take to smoke the food in Chapter 2, "Basic Recipes."

Making Sure It All Works: Professional Tips and Tricks for Smoking

Problem	Cause	What to do
Not enough smoke, the fuel goes out, or does not burn through.	The wood used is too damp.	Use dry fuel.
	The air vent is not open wide enough; there is not enough fresh air for the fuel to smolder.	You should be able to adjust the air vents gradually to improve smoke production.
Too much smoke, the fuel burns too quickly.	The fuel is packed too loosely or is too dry.	The fuel must be tightly packed to keep it from burning too fast.
The smoked food is too dry and develops a distinct outside layer.	Smoking temperature was too hot or storage was too warm and too dry.	Lower smoking temperature and improve storage conditions.
The smoked food begins to go moldy.	The smoked food was not brined long enough.	According to the amount, you could wash off the meat, smoke it again, and consume quickly.
	The meat was not pre-dried enough.	The meat must be completely dry before it is put into the smoker.
	Not smoked enough (the smoke ingredients gives it a preservative effect and inhibits mold growth).	Check how long you smoke the food; possibly provide more fresh air.
	The smoked food was stored too long in too damp a place.	Check the humidity in the storage room; it should not exceed 70% – air it more frequently anyway.
The smoked food spoils.	The pieces of food were hung too close together, so no smoke reached the places where they touched.	Always hang the pieces of food to be smoked far enough apart.
	Storeroom or aging room hygiene not up to standard.	Cleanliness is essential – the aging room must be aired often and the humidity checked regularly.
The smoked food drips melted fat.	Smoking temperature too high.	Monitor temperature regularly; be especially careful with fatty bacon.
Fish falls off the hooks.	The fish were not hung up the right way.	Use the right hooks, made for fish, and push them through correctly (see page 26).
	The fish are too heavy.	Fish pieces are too heavy; hang up the pieces separately (see page 26).
	You used frozen fish.	After salting, frozen fish is flakier than fresh, so place them on the hooks carefully.
The smoked food tastes strange (carbolic, turpentine, etc.).	Tainted fuel can cause unpleasant tastes (foreign components, paint residues, etc.).	Check the quality of your fuel.
	Fuel was stored in a too-damp place.	Store the fuel properly.

(Source: Qualitätshandbuch für Fleisch und Fleischerzeugnisse [Quality Control Manual for Meat and Meat Products], Vienna 2006)

Cure It First

Preparing Fish, Poultry, and Meat for Smoking

Preparing fish, meat, poultry, and anything else you might want to smoke is just as important as the choice of sawdust and keeping to the cooking time. Curing or salting is done, both to preserve the smoked food and because it improves the taste. Also important: salt draws moisture from the smoking food and anything you smoke must be as dry as possible when it is put into the smoker. When you cure or salt the food for smoking, this sets off a physical reaction scientifically called osmosis: the brine penetrates into the tissue and replaces the water with salt.

Salt is not just Salt

Curing salt is a mixture of approximately 99.6% sodium chloride and 0.4% sodium nitrite. It is used to prepare all types of hams and cured products, to ensure the keeping quality. Curing salt greatly inhibits growth of micro-organisms while also improving the taste. Mixing the curing salt with sugar (approximate amounts: for every ounce/kilogram curing salt, add two teaspoons or 10g of sugar) also gives the meat its characteristic red, appetizing color. A complicated biochemical process produces nitric acid; when this acid breaks down, this causes nitric oxide to form. When nitric oxide binds with the red meat pigment (myoglobin) to make nitrosomyoglobin, the meat will stay red after it is cooked. This chemical process is called reddening: Uncured meat turns gray when cooked while brined remains red to pink.

However, nitrite curing salt has a bad name — it is considered carcinogenic and is toxic in quantities of over 0.18 ounces (5g). Therefore, the legal limit is between approximately 1/1000 ounce to 3/1000 ounce per pound (or 50 and 250 milligrams per kilogram).

When nitrite combines with certain amino acids, nitrosamines, which are carcinogenic substances, can be formed. Brined meat and fish may contain traces of such nitrosamines. When brined or cured meat or fish is heated, this favors formation of nitrosamines. Larger amounts form at temperatures between 338–365°F (170-185°C). Therefore, it is advisable not to eat brined or cured and grilled meat too often. It is also better to only cold smoke or warm smoke cured meats.

You can usually buy curing salt at a butcher's supply store. You should not mix it yourself because the commercially available curing salt definitely has the right proportions, but you can add herbs and spices to taste, to give ham or goose breast a very special touch.

Dry Curing

In this technique, curing salt, herbs, spices, and some sugar (0.16 ounce per pound of salt [10 grams per kilogram]) are rubbed "dry" into the meat. Sugar helps the curing or marinating process and rounds out the taste, since it is the "nourishment" for the bacteria in the meat that creates the flavor.

Next, put the pieces on a rack and set it in a tub, so that the liquid that forms can drain off. Depending on the size of the pieces of meat, dry curing can take between 2 and 6 weeks and should be done at cool temperatures around 41°F (5°C). When it is completed, rinse the meat thoroughly; usually the meat is soaked in cold water for 8-10 hours, changing the water at least 2-3 times.

Now, dry off the food; it can be kept at a temperature 34-35°F (1-2°C) warmer, but humidity must never exceed 70%.

Wet Curing or Brining

As for dry curing, rub the pieces of meat with the curing salt mixture and then put them in layers in the brining tub. Pour over the prepared brine: do this carefully, so that the salt is not completely rinsed off the meat.

Wet curing or brining is especially recommended for smaller pieces of meat (such as rolled pork loin) and does not take as long as classic dry curing. The average time needed for brining depends on the size of the pieces and takes about a week. The ratio of the brine to meat is important: it should be 1:6 (1 quart of brine to 6 pounds of meat). If you use too much brine, you risk the food becoming over-salted, but using too little creates favorable conditions for unwanted bacteria.

TIP:

You can make a hygienic and safe brine by briefly boiling the brining liquid, mixed with the salt and spices, and allowing it to cool completely, before you pour it over the meat.

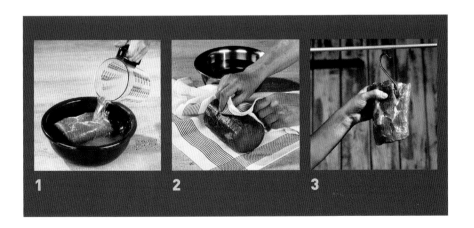

Brining a Rolled Pork Loin:
1. After rubbing the meat with the curing salt mixture and spices, put it in the brining liquid in an earthenware vessel.
2/3. After a brining time of 2-6 weeks, rinse the meat thoroughly and hang it in the fresh air.

Table Salt, Sea Salt, Rock Salt
Anyone who prefers to hot smoke their food should cure the fish and meat using table salt, sea salt, or rock salt — which one is up to you, but it should be without the additives used to make it easier to pour. Of course, you can mix the salt of your choice with spices and herbs. The osmosis process is the same as when using curing salt, but you get no reddening.

There are two ways to salt fish and meat

Fish is usually dry-salted. Rub the gutted and cleaned fish inside and outside with salt and then, depending on its size and weight, lay it in a tub for a few hours. This process may cause uneven concentrations of salt.

Wet salting or brining in a salt brine, however, ensures even amounts of salt in the fish. The guideline ratio for the salt solution is: 1/4 cup of salt (2 ounces or 60g) per 1 quart/liter water. For 2 pounds (1kg) of meat, you need about 1-1/2 quarts/liters

brine. The brine must cover the fish or meat completely; turn it several times during the process. After brining, you must throw away the liquid for hygienic reasons.

Even if you are certain you did everything right, the brine can spoil and the meat or fish with it. Reasons include:
• The salt concentration of the brine is not high enough
• Too much sugar in the brine
• The fish or meat were not fresh
• The crockery or cooking utensils were infected with bacteria
• Too high temperature during the brining process (in refrigerator or room)
   Therefore, buying a decoction meter is a good idea; it measures the exact concentration of the brine solution.

Preparing Fish
If you are going to smoke fish whole, they should be cut open lengthwise along the belly and the guts cut off from behind the head and removed in one piece, without cutting them open. Next, wash the fish carefully, preferably under running water. The blood should be carefully washed off and the fish must be de-slimed. The gills must be removed, because they provide a particularly good breeding ground for bacteria and often bleed, which causes ugly stripes during smoking. With eels, you can simply squeeze the gills out and remove them.

For larger fish, which are smoked in halves, cut the fish along the dorsal fin up to the spine and keep cutting up to the head. Cut from the spine to the tail and split along the tail fin. Next, take out the ribs using the knife point, but be sure not to cut into the guts while doing this. Now, carefully remove the entire innards, including the kidneys, but be careful not to cut into the gall bladder since this would spoil the whole fish. Split the head, preferably with a heavy knife, or if needed, use a bat or mallet. Be sure that the fish is still held together at the base of the gills. Now lay the fish halves open and carefully pull the guts out. Remove the gills (caution: you can hurt yourself) and wash the fish thoroughly. You may need to scrub them under running water with a tooth brush.

Important:

Whether you are dry or wet salting the fish, the tub must be kept in a dark and cool place (50-59°F or 10-15°C).

Tip:

When you are gutting the fish, never take hold of it by the gill openings: they are razor sharp and you can hurt yourself.

Tip:

Make sure that you do not cut too deeply with the knife, as you might cut into the intestines or gall bladder. If bile leaks out, it spoils the whole fish, giving it a bitter taste.

When you are smoking large fish, it is best to cut it into pieces.
Cut off the head using a slanting slice starting on the side of the belly behind the gills and then cut up to the backbone.

Sometimes — if the fish has a thick spine — it is best to cut into the backbone and twist off the head. Cut the fish carefully into pieces about the same size, and again be careful not to cut into the intestines or gall bladder, as already stated: bile spoils the taste. The kidneys lie along the backbone and must be fully removed. A toothbrush is also useful here. Now, remove the intestines carefully from the pieces and clean the fish thoroughly under running water.

Add the brine: For 10 pounds (5kg) of prepared fish, you need about 5 quarts/liters of brine. Boil 5 quarts/liters of water with about 1/4 cup (350-400g) of table salt, the juice of half a lemon, and dried herbs and spices (see information box on spices), and allow the whole to cool. Salt the fish well inside and out, and then put the fish into the cold (!) brine and leave it there for about 12 hours, turning it several times.

Air drying: After the brining, rinse the fish again thoroughly under running water, removing any remaining blood or slime, and then hang them up to dry or lay them on a rack. This drying process in the fresh air — ideally in a shady and breezy place — takes about 1-2 hours.

Tip:

If you are using saltwater fish, the brine can be somewhat less salty, because the fish has a stronger flavor of its own.

Tip:

Don't dry the fish in the sun to speed up the process; this has a big effect on the taste.

Oven drying: This method gives the fish a hot-dry pre-smoking: hang the fish in the smoker and dry it at a low temperature, at most 120°F (50°C), with only a small amount of smoke. Leave the smoker door slightly ajar, to ensure adequate air circulation. Make absolutely sure that the temperature rises slowly, since otherwise the fish will become too flaky and fall off the hooks. After about 30-60 minutes, the fish should be dry; they will also feel a bit leathery, but must not be sticky. Only now comes the actual smoking.

Only eels, eelpout, and garfish should be given a hot-wet pre-smoking. To do this, after thoroughly washing off the brine, season the fish with pepper and put it in the smoker, depending on the size, for 45-60 minutes at 195-210°F (90-100°C), with the door a little ajar.

Tip:

A good way to tell if the fish is cooked: if you can pull the dorsal fin out easily and the attached flesh is white, then the fish is ready to eat.

Two Steps for Smoking

There are two steps to smoking fish: the fish is first cooked at about 195-250°F (90-120°C); the actual smoking is the second step. Slowly reduce the temperature to about 140°F (60°C); the smoke increases, and this is what gives the fish its distinctive golden color. If you prolong the first phase to about 20 minutes, you can eat the fish immediately, although the smoked taste won't be as intense.

Frozen Fish

You can also smoke frozen fish. To ensure there is no loss of flavor, the frozen fish should be thawed as slowly as possible, ideally in the refrigerator. Once you can bend the fish, it is thawed enough. Now, salt it and hang it up to dry. After it has dried, smoke it just as you would fresh fish.

Note: Frozen fish absorbs salt very readily and, after it is brined, it is much flakier than fresh fish. It must be hung up carefully, or best, smoke it on a grill.

Preparing Meat and Poultry

As with preparing fish, it is a good idea to thoroughly salt meat or poultry before smoking it, which lends it much of the typical savory flavor.

If you want to hot smoke meat or poultry, rub it carefully with salt and spices (dry curing) and refrigerate it overnight. To ensure that everything is evenly salted, brine it (wet curing).

Before you smoke the meat or poultry, rinse it carefully and dry it using paper towels. Now, as you would for preparing fish, hang the food to be smoked in a well-ventilated and shady place.

If you want to cold smoke fish, meat, or poultry, you cannot omit curing it; otherwise the smoked food will spoil. Rub the meat thoroughly with curing salt. You can add spices to the salt (see information box). Lay the meat in a plastic bowl or earthenware pot and pour over the brine, which must cover the meat completely. It is best to put the covered bowl in the refrigerator; 39-40°F (4-5°C) is ideal. How long you keep the meat in the brine depends on size. If the curing process takes several days, skim off the foam, which forms everyday, to prevent growth of any unwanted bacteria.

Suggested brine mixture: Mix 1 quart/liter water with 1/3 cup (100g) curing salt, 2-1/2 teaspoons (10g) sugar, spices of your choice, and boil briefly. Let the brine cool before using it. Brining times: (these are approximate; the recipes give more exact times)

Meat	Wet-brining time	Drying time
For each pound (500g) of pork	4-6 days	1-2 days
For each pound (500g) of beef	5-7 days	1-2 days
For each pound (500g) of chicken	2-3 days	1-2 days
For each pound (500g) of venison	12 hours	1-2 days

Spices

When you cure meat, you can use all kinds of different spices and herbs to your taste (juniper berries, cloves, bay leaf, allspice, caraway, pepper, mace, marjoram, thyme, rosemary, etc.). You can also buy prepared spice mixtures. You can use herbs and spices whole, ground, or add them to the brine in small cotton bags. Never use your fingers to sprinkle the herbs and spices in the brine — always use a clean spoon. After usage, close the spice package immediately and store in a dry place. Make sure that any spices you use for curing or brining raw meat, poultry, or fish are as germ-free as possible. Herbs from your own garden are often full of germs that can harm the sensitive brining process. Therefore, always boil the brine mixture for a short time first.

Tip:

Cleanliness is crucial when curing food, to prevent growth of unwanted bacteria.

Basic Recipes for

Fish, Meat, Game, and Poultry

Basic Recipes for Fish

In principle, you can cold or hot smoke all salt and freshwater fish, either as whole fish, in halves, or as fillets or steaks. Fish with higher fat content, such as salmon, mackerel, or carp, stay juicier during smoking and are generally considered better-tasting. Low-fat fish, such as pike, perch, or zander (pikeperch), can get a bit dried out in the smoker. For these fish, it's important to pay close attention to timing while smoking. When smoking saltwater fish, the brine should contain less salt because the fish has a stronger flavor of its own. For the same reason, add smaller amounts of spices and herbs to saltwater fish. As already noted, the brine you use for frozen fish should also be a bit less concentrated because freezing changes the flesh structure and the fish absorbs more salt.

Hot smoking is more commonly used for fish, at least by hobby smokers. The usual method is to cook the whole fish in hot smoke at 140-250°F (60-120°C) for 60-90 minutes, depending on the size; this smokes them at the same time. You can also split up this process: First, cook the fish at about 195°F (90°C) for 20-40 minutes and then smoke it at about 120°F (50°C) for 45 minutes to two hours. When using either process, it's a good idea to briefly increase the temperature during the cooking time to 210-250°F (100-120°C). This destroys any bacteria still on the fish.

If you want to cold smoke, it is best to use fish halves, fillets, or steaks that have a higher fat content because the flesh will be drier, making it harder to remove the bones. There is no cooking phase in cold smoking, so the fish has to be preserved by other means: wet or dry curing or brining (see page 31). Depending on how thick the fillets are, put the brining tub in a cool place for 12-36 hours and then thoroughly rinse off the salt and sugar in cold water. Pat the fillets dry and hang them up to dry. The optimal temperature for cold smoking is between 60-75°F (15-25°C). Here, the time needed for smoking takes longer, depending on the size of food you are smoking.

Tip:
The fresher the fish, the better it tastes. Fishermen know this and prepare their catch for smoking immediately.

Tip:
The fish are ready-smoked when they have turned the typical golden smoked color and the back flesh is no longer too soft. It should feel as firm as the tip of your nose when you press it with your finger. If the fish feels more like your cheek, the flesh is still too soft and the fish has to be smoked longer.

Cold Smoked Fish

The suggested smoking or brining times are only approximate, depending on the size and thickness of the pieces and the different kind of equipment used. When the smoker has a thermostat, it is easy to control the temperature. If using a simpler smoker without a thermometer, you have to watch the color of the smoke during the process. The following rule of thumb goes for the smoke: It should be white and thick — if it turns gray-blue, add sawdust.

Freshwater Fish

Ingredients:
4 fish, 10-1/2 ounces
each (300g)

Smoking wood:
Alder sawdust;
you can also add
juniper berries,
dried bay leaves,
or lemon peel

Hot Smoked Trout, Char, and Whitefish
Here's how:
1. Brine the gutted and well-washed fish for about 10-12 hours: bring to a boil 2 quarts/liters of water with 1/2 cup (150g) of sea salt; you can add a little dill and crushed juniper berries. Let cool. (See page 34.)
2. Rinse the fish under running water and pat dry. Hang in a well-aired place to dry for about an hour.
3. Preheat the smoker and sawdust until the sawdust smolders. Place the fish on the oiled grill and slide it into the smoker at 210-250°F (100-120°C). Cook about 30 minutes and then reduce the temperature at about 120°F (50°C) and smoke the fish for 60-90 minutes.
4. Serve the fish warm with fresh salad and a baguette. (For other serving ideas, see recipes starting on page 62.)
5. If you want to cook and smoke at the same time, preheat the oven to 300-355°F (150-180°C) and then put the fish in the hot smoke for 20-25 minutes.

Hot Smoked Carp, Pike, Wels catfish, and Salmon

Here's how:

1. Split the gutted and washed fish lengthwise as described on page 33, and rinse again thoroughly. Brine them for about 10-12 hours: bring to a boil 3 quarts/liters of water with 3/4 cup (240g) of sea salt; you can add onions, crushed pepper, and fish spice mixture. Let cool. (See page 34.)

2. Rinse the fish under running water thoroughly and dry. Hang to dry in a well-aired place for about 1-2 hours.

3. Preheat the smoker with the sawdust until the sawdust smolders. Put the fish in the smoker and cook at 210-250°F (100-120°C) for about 45 minutes, and then reduce the temperature to about 120°F (50°C) and smoke the fish 60-90 minutes.

4. Serve the cooled fish with potato salad. (For other serving ideas, see recipes starting on page 62.)

5. If you want to cook and smoke at the same time, heat the oven to 300°F (150°C) and hang the fish in the hot smoke for 60 minutes.

Ingredients:
Either 4 fish halves
or cutlets
of 9 to 14 ounces
(250 to 400g)

Smoking wood:
Beech chips;
you can also add
juniper berries
or bay leaves

Ingredients:
4 eels, 12-14 ounces
each (350-400g)

Smoking wood:
Beech and
hickory chips

Hot-wet Smoked Eels

Here's how:

1. De-slime and gut the eels (use salt or bird sand), wash thoroughly as described on page 33, and brine them for approximately 10-12 hours: bring to a boil 5 quarts/ liters of water with 1 pound (500g) of sea salt; you can also add crushed pepper and juniper berries. Let cool. (See page 34.)

2. Rinse the eels carefully under running water and dip them briefly in boiling water to open the belly flaps.

3. Preheat the smoker and sawdust until the sawdust smolders. Put the still-wet eels in the smoker, making sure they don't touch, and cook according to weight, at 210-250°F (100-120°C) for about 25-40 minutes. Now, reduce the temperature to approximately 150°F (65°C), and smoke the fish for 90 minutes.

4. Cool the eels well — preferably overnight — so that the smoke flavor is evenly distributed and serve with rustic bread or use in other ways. (For other serving ideas, see recipes starting on page 62.)

Hot Smoked Perch, Bream, and Tench

Here's how:

1. Split the gutted and washed fish lengthwise as described on page 33, and rinse again thoroughly. Brine them for about 10-12 hours: bring to a boil 3 quarts/liters of water with 3/4 cup (240g) of sea salt; you can also add onion, crushed pepper, bay leaves, and lemon peel. Let cool. (See page 34.)
2. Rinse the fish under running water thoroughly and dry. Hang to dry in a well-aired place about 1-2 hours.
3. Preheat the smoker and sawdust until the sawdust smolders. Hang the fish in the smoker and cook at 210-250°F (100-120°C) for about 30-45 minutes, and then reduce the temperature to about 150°F (65°C) and smoke the fish for 90 minutes.
4. Serve the fish, either still warm or cooled, with fried potatoes and horseradish. (For other serving ideas, see recipes starting on page 62.)
5. If you want to cook and smoke at the same time, heat the oven to 300°F (150°C) and leave the fish in the hot smoke for one hour.

Ingredients:
4 fish halves of 7 to 10-1/2 ounces each (200-300g)

Smoking wood:
Beech chips; you can also add juniper berries, bay leaves, pepper, and dried lemon peel

Cold Smoked Salmon

Here's how:

1. Clean and wash the salmon as described on page 33, split lengthwise, bone it, and rinse again thoroughly. (You can also buy already prepared sides of salmon from your fishmonger.)
2. Mix 1 pound (450g) of coarse sea salt and one pound (450g) of cane sugar and, according to taste, add 10 crushed juniper berries, 10 peppercorns, and 1 bay leaf for a dry marinade. Lay the fish in a pan as long as the sides of the salmon and generously sprinkle with the marinade on both sides. The fish should be completely covered with the salt-sugar mixture.
3. Let the salmon rest for about 18 hours in a cold place, but always keep basting with the resulting liquid. Now, thoroughly rinse the fish, removing all the remaining salt and sugar, and pat dry.
4. Heat the smoker and bring 1 pound (450g) of beech smoking sawdust to a smolder. Reduce the heat to about 60°F (15°C) and hang the sides of salmon in the smoker. Smoke for 10-12 hours and then let stand for 10-12 hours. Repeat this process two more times.
5. The cold-smoked salmon can be served immediately with toast. (For other serving ideas, see recipes starting on page 62.)

Ingredients:
2 sides of salmon, 35 ounces each (1kg)

Smoking wood:
Beech chips, fruit tree shavings; you can also add peppercorns, juniper berries, and bay leaves

Saltwater Fish

Hot Smoked Sole, Plaice, and Flounder
Here's how:

Ingredients:
4 whole fish
10-1/2 to 14 ounces each
(300-400g)

Smoking wood:
Beech or alder sawdust;
you might add
juniper berries,
bay leaves,
peppercorns,
dried lemon

1. Have the fishmonger clean the fish; rinse them again and brine for about 8-10 hours: bring to a boil 2-1/2 quarts/liters of water with 7 tablespoons (125g) of sea salt; you can also add crushed pepper and lemon peel. Let cool. (See page 34.)
2. Rinse the fish carefully under running water and pat dry. Hang to dry in a well-aired place for about an hour.
3. Preheat the smoker and smoking sawdust until the sawdust smolders. Put the fish on the oiled grill, slide it into the smoker or hang the fish in the smoker, and cook at 210-250°F (100-120°C) for about 45 minutes. Now, reduce the temperature to about 165°F (75°C), and smoke the fish for 60-90 minutes.
4. Serve the cooled fish with mixed salad. (For other serving ideas, see recipes starting on page 62.)
5. If you want to cook and smoke at the same time, preheat the oven to 300-360°F (150-180°C) and then put the fish in the hot smoke for 1 hour.

Hot Smoked Halibut and Dogfish
Here's how:

Ingredients:
4 pieces of fish,
cutlets or fillets,
of 7 ounces each
(200g)

Smoking wood:
Beech and
hickory sawdust

1. Wash the kitchen-ready fish pieces and put in the brine for about 8-10 hours: bring to a boil 2 quarts/liters of water with 1/3 cup (100g) of sea salt; you can add crushed pepper, bay leaves, onion, herbs of your choice. Let cool. (See page 34.)
2. Rinse the fish carefully under running water and dry it off. Hang to dry in a well-aired place for about an hour.

The belly flaps or walls of the spiny dogfish are sold as "Schillerlocken" [Friedrich Schiller's curly locks] and the back pieces as "sea eel."

3. Preheat the smoker with the smoking sawdust until the sawdust smolders. Put the pieces of fish on the oiled grill, slide it into the smoker, and cook at 210-250°F (100-120°C) for about 45 minutes. Now, reduce the temperature to about 165°F (75°C) and smoke the fish for 60-90 minutes.
4. Serve the cooled pieces of fish with potato salad. (For other serving ideas, see recipes starting on page 62.)
5. If you want to cook and smoke at the same time, preheat the oven to 100-360°F (150-180°C) and then hang the fish in the hot smoke for 60 minutes.

Hot Smoked Redfish, Cod, and Haddock

Here's how:
1. Wash the kitchen-ready fish fillets and then brine them for about 6-8 hours: bring to a boil 2 liters of water with 1/3 cup (100g) of sea salt; you can also add crushed pepper, bay leaves, mustard seed, and lemon peel. Let cool. (See page 34.)
2. Rinse the fish carefully under running water and pat dry, and then hang to dry in a well-aired place for about 1-2 hours.
3. Preheat the smoker and sawdust until the sawdust begins to smolder. Put the fish on the oiled grill, slide it into the smoker, and cook it at 210-250°F (100-120°C) for about 45 minutes. Next, reduce the temperature to about 165°F (75°C) and smoke the fish pieces for 60 minutes.
4. Serve the cooled fish with a mixed salad. (For other serving ideas, see recipes starting on page 62.)
5. If you wish to smoke and cook the fish together, preheat the smoker to 100-360°F (150-180°C) and hang the fish in the hot smoke for 60 minutes.

Ingredients:
4-7 ounce fillets
(200g)

Smoking wood:
Beech or alder sawdust;
you can also add
crushed pepper,
bay leaves,
and dried lemon peel

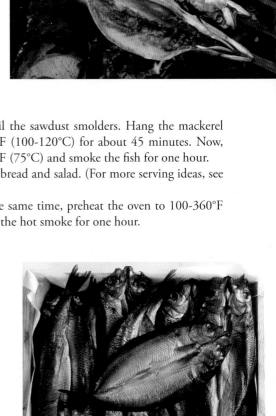

Ingredients:
4 mackerel of
14 to 16 ounces each
(400-450g)

Smoking wood:
Beech chips,
hickory sawdust

Hot Smoked Mackerel

Here's how:

1. Have the fishmonger clean the fish, rinse it again, and brine for about 6-8 hours: bring to a boil 4 quarts/ liters water with 2/3 cup (200g) of sea salt; you can also add crushed pepper, bay leaves, juniper berries, or lemon peel. Let cool. (See also "Spices," page 37.)

2. Rinse the fish carefully under running water and dry off, and then hang to dry in a well-aired place for about 1-2 hours.

3. Preheat the smoker and sawdust until the sawdust smolders. Hang the mackerel in the smoker and cook at 210-250°F (100-120°C) for about 45 minutes. Now, reduce the temperature to about 165°F (75°C) and smoke the fish for one hour.

4. Serve the cooled mackerel with rustic bread and salad. (For more serving ideas, see recipes starting on page 62.)

5. If you want to cook and smoke at the same time, preheat the oven to 100-360°F (150-180°C) and then put the fish in the hot smoke for one hour.

Ingredients:
4 herrings
of 1/2 pound each
(250g)

Smoking wood:
Alder sawdust;
you can also add
peppercorns
and bay leaves

Hot Smoked Green Herrings

Here's how:

1. Have the fishmonger prepare the fish, wash it again, and brine for about 4-5 hours: bring to a boil 2-1/2 quarts/ liters of water with 7 tablespoons (125g) sea salt, 2 tablespoons (25g) sugar, 1 tablespoon (20ml) vinegar; you can also add crushed pepper and bay leaves. Let cool. (See also "Spices," page 37.)

2. Rinse the fish carefully under running water and dry off, and then hang to dry in a well-aired place for about 1-2 hours.

3. Preheat the smoker and sawdust until the sawdust smolders. Put the fish on the oiled grill, slide it into the smoker, and smoke at 300°F (150°C) for about 1 hour. (For more serving ideas, see recipes starting on page 62.)

Green Herrings

The German name for green herrings, Bückling, probably comes from the word "pökeln" (pickle or cure): In parlance, the word "Pökeling" turned into "Bückling." The derogatory term "Bückling," which refers to the subservient officials, has nothing to do with green herrings. This term is derived from "sich bücken" (bend yourself over).

Hot Smoked Mussels

Here's how:

1. Wash the mussels under running water and brush them thoroughly. Discard any opened mussels and drain the rest in a colander. Do not marinate or brine them.
2. Put the mussels in a drip pan, pour on a cup of water, and drizzle on some olive oil.
3. Preheat the smoker and sawdust until the sawdust smolders.
4. Slide the drip pan into the smoker and smoke the mussels at 360°F (180°C) for about 45 minutes. Throw away any mussels that have not opened up.
5. Put the mussels in soup bowls and garnish with chopped parsley. Serve with a baguette.

Ingredients:
2 lbs (1kg) mussels,
1 cup white wine,
soup vegetables
Smoking wood:
Beech sawdust;
you can also add
bay leaves,
pepper, juniper,
and mustard seed

Hot Smoked Scallops

Here's how:

1. Wash the scallops, pat dry, and then dry marinate them for 20 minutes in the following: mix 2/3 cup (200g) coarse sea salt, 1/2 cup (100g) light brown sugar, and some grated and dried orange peel. Sprinkle over the scallops.
2. Wash off the marinade thoroughly, pat the scallops dry with paper towels, and then let dry for about an hour in a cool, well-ventilated room.
3. Prepare a wok or roasting pan (see page 27). Once the sawdust starts to smolder, lay the scallops on a piece of aluminum foil, put it on the grill, put the lid immediately back on, and smoke the scallops for six minutes.
4. Serve the smoked scallops with fennel salad and toast. (For other serving ideas, see recipes starting on page 62.)

Ingredients:
12 shelled scallops
Smoking wood:
Alder sawdust

Hot Smoked Shrimp, Scampi, and Crayfish

Here's how:

1. Wash, peel, and pat dry the shellfish. Do not marinate or brine them.
2. Prepare a wok or roasting pan (see page 27) and, once to the sawdust begins to smolder, put the shrimp, scampi, or crayfish on a piece of aluminum foil on the grill, replace the cover immediately, and smoke the shellfish for 6 minutes.
3. Serve the smoked shrimp, scampi, or crayfish with aioli sauce and toast or in a fish soup. (For other serving ideas, see recipes starting on page 62.)

Ingredients:
20 raw shellfish
Smoking wood:
Alder sawdust

Basic Recipes for Meat, Game, and Poultry

Besides warm smoking, which is mainly used in industrial food preparation, there are two ways to smoke meat, poultry, and game: either cold or hot.

The main difference between the two methods is that cold smoking meat (poultry, game), does not cook it. Therefore, the smoked product must be cured or brined beforehand. Both methods already help preserve the food. After it is cured, the meat (poultry, game) is no longer quite raw; it has more flavor and keeps longer. To smoke it afterwards, first dry the food; this "relaxes," or tenderizes, the meat and creates a firmer skin or rind. How long the drying takes depends on the size of the pieces; it can be up to 24 hours. Since the meat (poultry, game) is only exposed to cold smoke and isn't heated, this process takes much longer than hot smoking, sometimes even several weeks.

In contrast to cold smoking, the meat (poultry, game) is cooked during hot smoking. The higher the temperature of the smoke, the shorter the smoking time. Hot smoking by itself does not make the meat (poultry, game) keep any longer; for that, it must first be cured or brined.

Carefully measure the amounts of wood chips or shavings you use. Too much can easily result in an "over-smoked" taste. The thinner the shavings, the faster they burn and the faster the smoke develops. Therefore, it is best to use sawdust, wood chips, or finely chopped twigs. Mixing different woods can sometimes give very good flavor results. Spices, tea, nut shells, etc. (see page 21) can also improve the taste. Our recipes are only suggestions; you will discover yourself over time which smoker you want to use, as well as which wood and smoking method, to smoke any particular piece of meat. Just as in cooking, when you're smoking food, creativity is also in demand.

Tip:

Don't brine or cure the meat too much. The heat of the smoke will intensify the salty flavor..

> **We recommend again: Keep your own food smoking log (smoking time, amount and type of wood used, temperature, herbs and spices used). This is the way you will quickly learn what tastes best to you. See sample log pages at the back of this book.**

Pork

Ingredients:
4 pieces
each 7 ounces
(200g)

Smoking wood:
Alder sawdust
with walnut shells;
you can also add
cinnamon sticks,
peppercorns,
or juniper berries

Hot Smoked Pork Cutlets and Fillet

Here's how:

1. Combine 1 quart/liter water, 1/3 cup (100g) of sea salt, 10 crushed white peppercorns, some dried orange zest, and the leaves from a thyme twig. Bring the brine to a boil, cool well, and add the meat for 2 hours. (See also page 36.)
2. Rinse off the marinade thoroughly, pat the meat dry with paper towels, and let it dry for about 3 hours in a cool, well-ventilated place.
3. Prepare a wok or roasting pan (see page 27) and, once the sawdust begins to smolder, lay the cutlets or fillet on the grill, cover immediately, and smoke the meat for about 20 minutes.
4. Alternatively, you can also put the meat on the oiled grill of the preheated smoker and smoke at 300°F (150°C) for 25 minutes.
5. Serve with salad or prepared vegetables. (For more serving ideas, see recipes starting on page 78.)

Ingredients:
4 pieces
each 7 ounces
(200g)

Smoking wood:
Beech and
plum tree chips;
you can also add
crushed peppercorns,
juniper berries,
and coriander

Hot Smoked Pork Chops and Neck Steak

Here's how:

1. Make a brine of 1-1/2 quarts/liters water, 1/2 cup (150g) of sea salt, 1 tablespoon crushed white peppercorns, 1 tablespoon juniper berries, and the leaves of a rosemary sprig. Bring to a boil, let it cool well, and add the meat for 2 hours. (See also page 36.)
2. Rinse off the marinade thoroughly, pat the meat dry with paper towels, and then let the meat dry for about 3 hours in a cool, well-ventilated place.
3. Prepare a wok or roasting pan (see page 27) and, once the sawdust begins to smolder, put the cutlet or fillet steak on the grill, close the lid immediately, and smoke the meat about 30 minutes.

4. You can also put the meat on the oiled grill of the preheated smoker and smoke it at 300°F (150°C) for 30 minutes.

5. Serve with salad or prepared vegetables. (For more serving ideas, see recipes starting on page 78.)

Hot Smoked Boneless Pork Shoulder

Here's how:

1. Wash the meat and pat dry. Crush 3 bay leaves, 1 tbsp caraway seeds, and 20 peppercorns in a mortar and mix with 1/3 cup (100g) of salt and 2 tsp of cane sugar (see page 36). Rub the meat with this mixture thoroughly and put it into a suitably-sized metal bowl. Cover the bowl well and let the meat marinade for 10 days in the refrigerator. This produces its own brine; turn the pork shoulder in this brine several times.

2. Take the meat out of the brine and rinse thoroughly; soak it for 8 hours, replacing the water several times, and then dry off the shoulder with paper towels and hang it up to dry for 24 hours in a cool, well-ventilated place.

3. Heat the smoker and sawdust or chips until smoldering. Hang the shoulder in the smoker or place on a grill and cook it at 195°F (90°C) for about 60-90 minutes.

4. Either serve warm, or let it cool and slice it like ham.

Cold Smoked Pork Tenderloin

Here's how:

1. Wash the meat and pat dry. Crush 3 bay leaves, 20 juniper berries, and 20 white peppercorns in a mortar and mix with 2 tbsp (50g) of salt and 1 tsp cane sugar (see page 36). Rub this into the meat thoroughly and place in a metal bowl. Cover the bowl well and let the meat marinate for 6 days in the refrigerator. Turn it repeatedly in the resulting brine.

2. Take out the pork tenderloin, rinse it thoroughly, and soak for 6 hours, changing the water several times.

3. Dry the meat with paper towels and hang it up for 10-12 hours to dry in a cool, well-ventilated place.

4. Heat the smoker and bring plenty of wood shavings to a smolder. Now, reduce the heat to about 60°F (15°C) and hang the pork loin in the smoker. Smoke for 8-10 hours and then let it rest for 10-12 hours. Repeat this process four more times.

5. Before eating the cold-smoked pork tenderloin, let it hang for 4-5 days in a cool, well-ventilated place to ripen and then slice. (For more serving ideas, see recipes starting on page 78.)

Ingredients:
4-1/2 pounds (2kg) pork shoulder

Smoking wood:
Alder and apple wood shavings

Ingredients:
2-1/4 pounds (1kg) pork tenderloin

Smoking wood:
Beech and hickory chips; you can also add juniper berries and bay leaves

Beef

Ingredients:
6-1/2 pounds (3kg)
beef brisket
(have the butcher
remove the fat
except for a thin layer)
Smoking wood:
Beech and
mesquite chips

Hot Smoked Beef Brisket Texas Style
Here's how:
1. Score the layer of fat on the brisket as for a pork roast. First, rub all over with 2 tablespoons mustard and then gently rub in a spice mixture of 2 tablespoons salt, 2 tablespoons brown sugar, 2 teaspoons ground black pepper, 2 tablespoons paprika, and 1 teaspoon chili powder. Put the brisket on a rack in a shallow roasting pan and let rest for 30 minutes.
2. Get the charcoal burning in a kettle grill with a temperature gauge and add smoking wood until white ash forms. When the grill reaches 250°F (120°C), put the brisket on the grill and close the lid immediately. Smoke at a temperature of 210-250°F (100-120°C) for 9 hours (3 hours per pound).
3. Wrap the brisket in aluminum foil and let it rest for about 30 minutes. Serve with mixed salad.

Ingredients:
4 fillets
each 7 ounces
(200g)
Smoking wood:
Beech sawdust,
walnut shells

Hot Smoked Beef Tenderloin
Here's how:
1. Put 3-4 tablespoons sawdust in the smoker and heat to 210°F (100°C).
2. Rub the slices of beef fillet with lemon pepper and salt. Heat oil in a frying pan and sear the fillet slices on each side for 1-2 minutes.
3. Put the fillets on the oiled grill of the smoker and smoke them for 15-20 minutes.
4. Serve with salad or prepared vegetables. (For more serving ideas, see recipes starting on page 78.)

Ingredients:
1 beef tenderloin,
about 4 pounds (2kg)
Smoking wood:
Beech and
mesquite shavings

Cold Smoked Beef Tenderloin
Here's how:
1. Make a dry marinade of 2 tablespoons (35g) sea salt, 1 teaspoon cane sugar, 20 crushed mixed peppercorns, 1 crumbled bay leaf, and 3 crushed juniper berries, and rub into the beef tenderloin.
2. Either put in a metal bowl and cover with foil or shrink-wrap the whole fillet using a vacuum-packing machine. Leave the fillet in the refrigerator for 8-10 days. If using a bowl, keep turning the fillet.
3. Take the tenderloin out of the bowl or remove it from the vacuum seal and hang it to dry for 3-4 days in a cool, well-ventilated place.
4. Soak for 2-1/2 hours, dry it off, and again let it cool and dry for two days.
5. Smoke the fillet in the smoker at 50-60°F (10-15°C) for 8-10 hours. Now, allow it to rest for 10 hours. Repeat this process 6 times.
6. When it is finished smoking, hang the fillets up again in a well-ventilated, cool place for another 10 days to mature. (For serving ideas, see recipes starting on page 78.)

Lamb

Hot Smoked Lamb Fillet

Here's how:

1. Make a brine of 1 quart/liter water, 1/3 cup (100g) of sea salt, 10 crushed white peppercorns, and the leaves from a sprig of thyme; bring it to a boil and allow to cool well (see page 36). Add the meat for 2 hours.
2. Rinse off the marinade thoroughly, pat the meat dry with paper towels, and then let dry for two hours in a cool, well-ventilated place.
3. Prepare a wok or roasting pan (see page 27) and, once the sawdust begins to smolder, lay the fillets on the grill, close the lid immediately, and smoke the meat for about 20 minutes.
4. You can also put the meat on the oiled grill of the preheated smoker and smoke at 300°F (150°C) for 20 minutes.
5. Serve with mixed salad. (For other serving ideas, see recipes starting on page 78.)

Ingredients:
4 lamb fillets
each 7 ounces
(200g)
Smoking wood:
Olive or walnut sawdust;
you can also
add rosemary

Hot Smoked Shoulder of Lamb

Here's how:

1. Wash the lamb shoulder and pat dry. Crush the needles of 3 sprigs of rosemary, 2 garlic cloves, and 20 peppercorns in a mortar, and mix with 1/3 cup (100g) of salt and 2 teaspoons cane sugar (see page 36). Rub the meat thoroughly with this mixture and put it in a metal bowl large enough to hold it. Cover the bowl carefully and marinate the meat for 24 hours in the refrigerator.
2. Wash the meat thoroughly under running water, dry with paper towels, and then hang to dry for 2-3 hours in a cool, well-ventilated place.
3. Heat the smoker and wood shavings until smoldering. Hang the lamb shoulder in the smoker or place it on a grill and smoke it at 210°F (100°C) for about 2-1/2 hours.
4. Serve with grilled tomatoes and bean salad. (For more serving ideas, see recipes starting on page 78.)

Ingredients:
3 pounds (1-1/2kg)
lamb shoulder
Smoking wood:
Beech and plum
tree chips
you can also add
rosemary

Game

Hot Smoked Saddle of Hare

Ingredients:
1 saddle of hare,
approximately 1-1/2 lbs
(600g)

Smoking wood:
Beech and
cherry sawdust;
you can also add
juniper berries
and bay leaves

Here's how:

1. Mix 3-1/2 ounces (100g) of sea salt, 1/3 cup (100g) of cane sugar, 10 coarsely ground white peppercorns, 5 crushed juniper berries, and some dried orange peel; rub this thoroughly into the meat and let marinate in the refrigerator for 45 minutes (see page 36).
2. Carefully rinse off the marinade, pat the meat dry with paper towels, and then dry for about 2 hours in a cool, well-ventilated place.
3. Put the saddle of hare on the oiled grill. Put the sawdust in the smoker. As soon as it smolders, slide in the hare and smoke it at 300°F (150°C) for 25 minutes.
4. Serve with hash browns and cranberry sauce. (For more serving ideas, see recipes starting on page 104.)

Hot Smoked Saddle of Venison Steaks and Venison Fillet Steaks

Ingredients:
4 fillets
5-7 ounces each
(150-200g)

Smoking wood:
Beech and
vine wood sawdust;
you can also add
juniper berries

Here's how:

1. Rub a marinade made of 1/3 cup (100g) of salt, 1/2 cup cane sugar, 2 crushed bay leaves, lemon pepper, and salt into slices of fillet, and let stand for 1 hour in the refrigerator. (See also page 36.)
2. Rinse off the marinade thoroughly, pat the meat dry with paper towels, and then let the meat dry for about 3 hours in a cool, well-ventilated place.
3. Put 4-5 tablespoons smoking sawdust into the smoker and heat it to 300°F (150°C). Put the fillets on the oiled grill of the smoker and, depending on the weight, smoke for 15-20 minutes.
4. Serve with salad or prepared vegetables. (For more serving ideas, see recipes starting on page 104.)

Poultry

Hot Smoked Whole Chicken

Ingredients:
1 chicken,
about 2-1/2 pounds
(1,200g)

Smoking wood:
Beech and apple
wood shavings

Here's how:

1. Make a brine of 2 quarts/liters of water, 3 bay leaves, 20 peppercorns, with 2/3 cup (200g) of salt and 2 teaspoons cane sugar, and bring it to a boil. Allow to cool. (See page 36.) Put the cold brine into a bowl.
2. Wash the chicken, pat dry, and leave it in the brine for 24 hours in the refrigerator. Take it out and rinse thoroughly under running water. Dry it with paper towels and hang it up for 24 hours to dry in a cool, well-ventilated place.

3. Heat the smoker with the wood shavings until they smolder. Hang the chicken in the smoker or lay it on a grill and cook it at 160-175°F (70-80°C) for 60-90 minutes, and then smoke it at 120°F (50°C) for 90 minutes.
4. Remove the leathery skin and serve the still-warm chicken with potato salad. (For more serving ideas, see recipes starting on page 96.)

Hot Smoked Chicken Breasts and Legs
Here's how:
1. Mix 1/3 cup (100g) of sea salt, 1 teaspoon of cane sugar, 10 crushed white peppercorns, a little dried orange peel, and leaves from a sprig of thyme into a dry marinade. Rub into the chicken breasts (see page 36). Let stand for one hour.
2. Rinse off the marinade thoroughly, pat the meat dry with paper towels, and then let dry for an hour in a cool, well-ventilated place.
3. Prepare a wok or roasting pan (see page 27). As soon as the sawdust begins to smolder, put the chicken breasts on the grill, cover immediately, and smoke the meat about 30 minutes.
4. Alternatively, the meat can be put on the oiled grill of the preheated smoker and smoked at 300°F (150°C) for 25-30 minutes.
5. Serve with mixed salad. (For more serving ideas, see recipes starting on page 96.)

Ingredients:
4 chicken breasts, skinless,
5 ounces each (150g)

Smoking wood:
Apple tree sawdust; you can also add juniper berries

Hot Smoked Turkey Legs
Here's how:
1. Wash the turkey legs and pat dry. Crush 3 bay leaves, mixed herbs (such as 3 sprigs each of thyme, sage, and oregano), 1 clove of garlic, and 20 peppercorns in a mortar and then mix with 2 tablespoons (50g) of salt and 1 teaspoon of cane sugar (see page 36). Rub the mixture all over the drumsticks and put them in a metal bowl. Cover the bowl carefully and let the meat marinate for 3-4 days in the refrigerator. Turn it repeatedly in the resulting brine.
2. Take out the drumsticks, rinse them, and soak two hours, changing the water several times. Finally, dry off the legs and let them air dry for 2-3 hours in a cool, well-ventilated place.
3. Bring the wood shavings to a smolder in the smoker, and cook the legs for 1 hour at 210°F (100°C) and then smoke them at 120°F (50°C) for about 90 minutes.
4. Before serving, remove the leathery skin. (For more serving ideas, see recipes starting on page 96.)

Ingredients:
2 turkey legs
14 ounces each (400g)

Smoking wood:
Cherry wood shavings

Chapter 2

Ingredients:
4 duck breasts
7 ounces each
(200g)

Smoking wood:
Beech sawdust
with black tea;
you can also add
cinnamon sticks,
and peppercorns

Hot Smoked Duck Breasts

Here's how:

1. Score the skin of the duck breasts and lay them on the oiled grill of the wok.
2. Prepare a wok or roasting pan (see page 27). Once the sawdust begins to smolder, place the duck breast on the grill. Close the lid immediately and smoke the meat for about 20 minutes.
3. Sauté the duck briefly on the skin side in a pan with a little olive oil until crisp.
4. Serve with lentil salad. (For more serving ideas, see recipes starting on page 96.)

Ingredients:
1 whole boneless
goose breast,
about 2 pounds
(1kg)

Smoking wood:
Beech and
juniper shavings

Cold Smoked Goose Breasts

Here's how:

1. Fold the goose breast over the inner sides and tie it up or put in a roasting net. Mix 4 teaspoons (30g) of sea salt, 1 teaspoon cane sugar, 20 crushed peppercorns, and 5 coriander seeds into a dry marinade, and gently rub it into the goose breast.
2. Either put the breast in a metal bowl and cover with foil, or shrink-wrap the whole breast using a vacuum-packing machine. Leave the breast for 8-10 days in the refrigerator. Turn the goose breast in the bowl several times.
3. Take the breast out of the bowl or cut off the shrink-wrapping and hang it up to mature for 3-4 days in a cool, well-ventilated place.
4. Now, soak for 2-1/2 hours. Dry it off, and again let it cool and dry for two days.
5. Put goose breast in the smoker and smoke it at 50-60°F (10-15°C) for 10 hours. Let it rest for 10 hours. Repeat this process 2 more times. (For serving ideas, see recipes starting on page 96.)

... and Whatever Else You Can Smoke

Cold Smoked Eggs

Here's how:
1. Boil the eggs, let cool, and then peel.
2. Put the eggs on the grill of the smoker and cold smoke them for 12 hours at approximately 70°F (20°C). (For more serving ideas, see recipes starting on page 108.)

Ingredients:
6 hard boiled eggs
Smoking wood:
Beech shavings

Cold Smoked Cheese

Here's how:
1. Sprinkle slices of semi-hard cheese on both sides with herbs of your choice. Pat dry feta and mozzarella slices, and also sprinkle with herbs or spices.
2. Put the cheese slices on a rack or grill and cold smoke them for 10 hours in the smoker at 75-85°F (25-30°C). You may turn them once. (For more serving ideas, see recipes starting on page 108.)

Ingredients:
Semi-hard cheese, such as Baby Swiss, Cheddar, Monterey Jack, Emmentaler, and some Goudas (you can also smoke feta and mozzarella), cut into 3/4" thick (2cm) slices
Smoking wood:
Beech shavings

Curing Salts

When you are cold smoking cheese, you can also make curing salts at the same time. Put about 2 pounds (1kg) coarse sea salt in a shallow aluminum pan and smoke the salt at the same time as the cheese.

Cold Smoked Tofu

Here's how:
1. Cut the tofu, just like the cheese, into 3/4" thick (2cm) slices, lay on a smoker grill, and cold smoke at 75-85°F (25-30°C) for about 8-10 hours. (For more serving ideas, see recipes starting on page 108.)

Hot Smoked Garlic

Here's how:
1. Preheat the smoker to 360°F (180°C). Rub the garlic generously with olive oil, put on a grill, and slide into the smoker.
2. Smoke the bulbs for about 45 minutes. (For more serving ideas, see recipes starting on page 108.)

Ingredients:
4 whole, intact garlic bulbs
Smoking wood:
Beech sawdust

Hot Smoked Almonds and Nuts

Here's how:
1. Preheat smoker to 165°F (75°C). Put the almonds or nuts, still in their shells, in a shallow aluminum pan, slide it into the smoker, and hot smoke for about 3 hours.
2. While still hot, sprinkle with sea salt and let cool.

Ingredients:
1/2 pound (250g) of un-shelled almonds or nutmeats
Smoking wood:
Beech sawdust

Chapter 3
Recipes
Using Smoked Ingredients

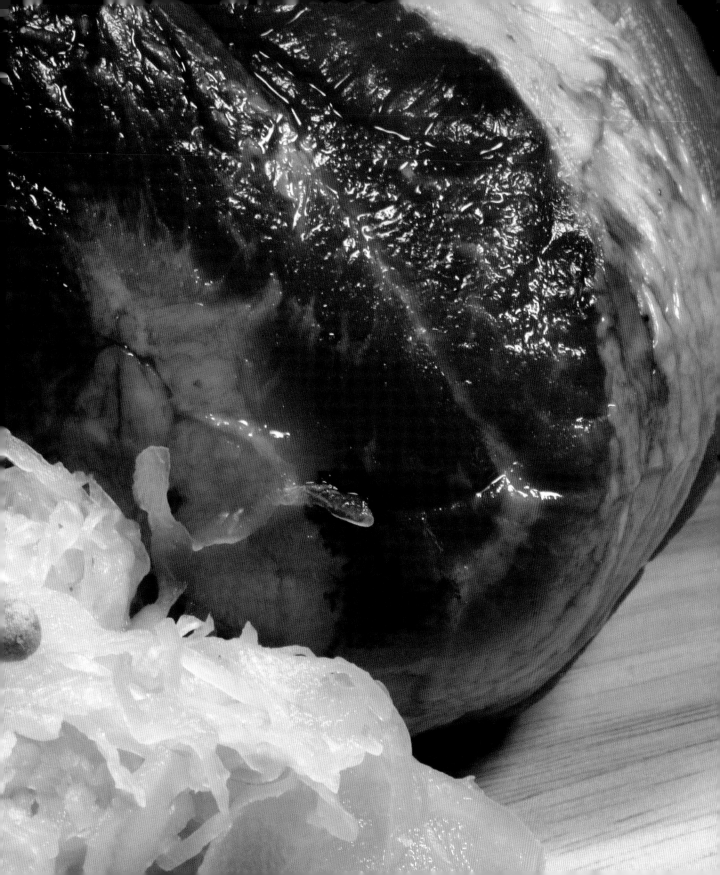

Fish, Shellfish, and Seafood

Crepes Filled with Smoked Trout

4 servings
3/4 cup (100g) flour
1/2 cup (130ml) milk
Salt
3 eggs
3 tbsp butter, softened
1 bunch of parsley
5 ounces (150g) smoked trout fillet (see page 42)
3/4 cup (150g) crème fraîche
1/2 cup (100g) yogurt
1 tbsp lemon juice
Lemon pepper
1 tsp olive oil

• Mix a smooth batter from the flour, milk, and a pinch of salt. Mix in eggs and butter and let the batter rest for 15 minutes.
• Wash the parsley, pat dry, and chop. Cut the smoked trout into pieces. Now, blend the crème fraîche with the yogurt, lemon juice, lemon pepper, and puree with the fish. Fold the parsley into the mixture and salt carefully. Heat the olive oil in a small non-stick pan and spoon in 1–2 tbsp crêpe batter. Fry a thin crêpe over medium heat. Make another seven the same way.
• Spread the crêpes with the crème fraîche-trout mixture and roll them up. Cut the rolls in half and serve, garnished with the remaining parsley.

Variation: Instead of smoked trout fillets, you can also use smoked mackerel fillets.

Smoked Whitefish Patties

4 servings
1-1/2 pounds (700g) smoked whitefish fillets (see page 42)
3/4 cup (80g) breadcrumbs
1/2 cup (100g) mayonnaise
2/3 cup (100g) shallots
Salt
Lemon pepper
3 tbsp oil
1 lemon cut in wedges

• Chop the fish very finely in a food processor or with a large knife. Mix bread crumbs and mayonnaise in a bowl.
• Peel the shallots and dice finely. Combine the mayonnaise mixture and shallots with the fish and mix well. Season with salt and lemon pepper to taste. • Make eight fish patties with the mixture, and then heat the oil in a frying pan and cook the patties on each side about 5 minutes until golden brown. Keep the finished patties warm.
• Serve with potato salad and lemon wedges.

Variation: Instead of smoked whitefish, use smoked cod and add 1 tsp. mustard to the fish mixture.

Baked Smoked Salmon

4 servings
14 ounces (400g) tomatoes
1 bunch basil
2 mozzarella balls
4 tbsp olive oil
White pepper
1 clove of garlic
1-1/2 lbs (600g) hot smoked salmon
(see page 43)
Oil for the baking dish

• Preheat the oven to 360°F (180°C). Pat the tomatoes dry and cut into slices. Wash the basil and shake dry; coarsely chop the leaves. Put both in a bowl, sprinkle on 2 tbsp of oil, season with pepper, and mix. Cut the mozzarella into very small pieces.
• Cut the garlic clove in half and rub a casserole dish, about 10" x 8" (25x20cm), with the cut surfaces of the garlic and then oil the dish. Pepper the fish fillets on both sides and put them in the dish. Pour the tomato mixture over the fish, sprinkle on the cheese, and drizzle on the remaining oil.
• Bake in the oven at 360°F (180°C) on the middle rack for 10-15 minutes. Serve with a baguette.

Variation: Also very tasty made with fillet of sole.

Smoked Salmon on Wasabi Vegetables

4 servings
1/2 lb (200g) carrots
1/2 lb (200g) celery
1 medium potato
1-1/2 tbsp (20g) butter
3/4 cup (200ml) vegetable stock
2 tsp wasabi
1 tbsp cream
1-1/2 lbs (600g) cold smoked salmon
(see page 45)
1 bag of potato chips

• Wash the carrots, celery, and potato. Peel the carrots and then cut the celery and carrots into thin strips.
• Peel the potato and chop into small pieces.
• Melt the butter in a small saucepan, sauté the vegetables, add the vegetable stock, and cook 15 minutes. Carefully pour off the vegetable stock while reserving 2-3 tbsp.
• Mix the wasabi with the vegetable stock and cream, and stir into the vegetables.
• Arrange the smoked salmon and wasabi vegetables onto four plates and serve each with a small portion of potato chips.

Smoked Shrimp Skewers with Tomato Sauce and Pesto

4 servings
3 bunches of basil
2 garlic cloves
1/2 cup (60g) grated parmesan or pecorino
1/2 cup (60g) pine nuts
1/3 cup (100ml) olive oil
1 tsp salt
12 fresh giant shrimp
12 sausage slices
1 pound (500g) firm tomatoes
Basil
1/4 cup (50ml) olive oil
Salt
Black pepper
A few drops lemon juice
4 wooden skewers

• Wash the basil, pat dry, and pull off the leaves; chop a third of them and set aside. Peel the garlic and coarsely chop. Put both, with the grated cheese and half the olive oil, into a blender jar. Puree mixture with a hand blender and gradually add the remaining oil.
• Wash the tomatoes, pat dry, and cut into small cubes. Drizzle with the olive oil, season with salt and pepper, and add the lemon juice. Add the remaining basil to the tomato mixture.
• Put four shrimp and four slices of sausage alternately on the skewers and smoke them in a wok for 4 minutes (see page 27).
• Put the tomato sauce on four plates, place the skewers on top, pouring a little pesto over each, and serve with a fresh baguette.

Variation: Instead of smoked shrimp, you can also use smoked scallops.

Smoked Scampi on Asparagus Risotto

4 servings
For the Risotto:
2 shallots
3/4 cup (150g) risotto rice
1-1/2 tbsp (20g) butter
1/3 cup (100ml) dry white wine
2 cups (500ml) chicken stock
1 pound (500g) green asparagus
1 tbsp olive oil
1/3 cup (40g) parmesan
1–2 drops of lemon juice
12 fresh smoked scampi (see page 49)

• Wash the asparagus, peel the lower third of the stalks, and trim off the ends. Cut the asparagus into bite-size pieces. Peel the shallots and chop into small pieces.
• Cook with the risotto rice in butter until it becomes translucent.
• Pour in the wine and let it cook down.
• Over medium heat, add the chicken stock, stirring constantly, and again let it cook down. After half the cooking time, add the asparagus and cook together.
• When the stock has reduced, take the pot off the stove, stir in the olive oil, cover, and let stand about 5 minutes.
• Fold in the grated cheese (Parmesan), and serve the risotto on four plates with the scampi on top.

Variation: This dish is also good using crayfish.

Smoked Eel
on Bean Salad

Four Servings
3/4 cup (100g) of green beans
Salt
3/4 cup (150g) broad beans
4 sprigs flat-leaf parsley
4 spring onions
2 tbsp sherry vinegar
2 tsp Dijon mustard
4 tbsp olive oil
Black pepper
4 tbsp chicken stock (jar)
1 pinch of sugar
1 smoked eel (see page 44)

• Wash the green beans, clean them, and cut into pieces about 1-1/2" (4cm) long. Cook in boiling salted water for 12 minutes; then refresh in ice water, drain, and place in a bowl.
• Peel the broad beans, cook in boiling salted water for 5 minutes, drain, and add to the green beans.
• Wash the parsley, shake dry, and coarsely chop. Also wash the spring onions, trim them, and cut into rings; add to the beans and mix everything together.
• Make vinaigrette of sherry vinegar, mustard, olive oil, salt, and pepper. Mix with chicken stock and sugar to taste and pour over the beans. Mix carefully.
• Arrange the bean salad on four plates. Cut the eel into four pieces, skin them, and arrange on the beans. Sprinkle with the chopped parsley.

Variation: Instead of smoked eel, you can also use smoked dogfish or smoked halibut.

Smoked Scallops
with Mango Salsa

Four Servings
12 fresh smoked scallops (see page 49)
1 ripe mango
1 small cucumber
1/2 red onion
1 hot green chili pepper
1 bunch of cilantro
3 tbsp freshly squeezed lime juice
Salt
Pepper

• Cut the mango in half and remove the core. Peel the cucumber, cut in half, and remove the seeds with a teaspoon. Chop the onion, mango, and cucumber into small, roughly same-size, cubes. Put everything in a small bowl.
• Wash the chili pepper, cut in half, remove the seeds and stem, and chop very finely. Wash the coriander, pat dry, and chop the leaves finely. Stir both into the mango mixture, add the lime juice, and season to taste with salt and pepper.
• Spread the salsa on four plates and arrange three scallops on each plate.

Smoked Herring
with Green Beans

Four Servings
1-1/2 (200g) green beans
1 shallot
1-1/2 tbsp (20g) butter
1 cup (250ml) vegetable stock
2 tbsp dark balsamic vinegar
2 tbsp beef stock (from a jar or use a cube)
1/2 tbsp olive oil
Pepper
1-4/5 ounces (50g) of bacon
4 fresh smoked herrings (see page 48)
1/2 bunch parsley
Olive oil

• Wash the beans and pat dry. Cut the shallot into small cubes and sauté in butter. Add the beans, pour in the vegetable stock, and let cook for 10 minutes. Drain and let cool slightly.
• Make vinaigrette of balsamic vinegar, oil, and pepper, pour over the warm beans, and mix.
• Cut the bacon into thin strips and let it render in a pan. Pour off the fat and mix the bacon strips with the cooled beans.
• Wash the parsley, pat dry, and chop the leaves. Divide the beans among four plates.
• Drizzle the herrings with a little olive oil and arrange atop the beans; garnish with chopped parsley.

Smoked Red Mullet
on Mixed Salad

Four Servings
2/3 cup (200g) coarse sea salt
1/2 cup (100g) light cane sugar
Dried peel of 1 lemon
1 tsp crushed fennel seeds
1 tsp crushed peppercorns
1 package mixed salad leaves (washed)
3 tbsp dark balsamic vinegar
3 tbsp chicken stock
1 tbsp olive oil
Salt
Lemon pepper
3-1/2 ounces (100g) seedless grapes
2 tbsp pistachios
8 fresh red mullet fillets

• Mix the sea salt, cane sugar, the dried lemon peel, fennel seeds, and peppercorns. Pour over the red mullet fillets. Cover with foil and let marinate for about 40 minutes.
• Wipe off the salt and rinse the fillets well under running water. Pat dry and then let dry for one hour in a cool, well-ventilated place. Smoke the red mullet for about 10 minutes in a wok (see page 27).
• Put the salad in a bowl and make vinaigrette of balsamic vinegar, chicken stock, olive oil, salt, and lemon pepper. Pour over the salad.
• Wash the grapes, pat dry, and then halve or quarter them. Sprinkle the pistachios over the salad. Divide the salad on four plates and arrange the smoked fish fillets on top.

Tip: This salad works well with any smoked fish.

Meat

Smoked Pork Tenderloin with Cabbage

(From Majorcan Cuisine)

Six Servings
1 cabbage
2 lbs. (1kg) smoked pork tenderloin (see page 53)
black pepper
7 ounces (200g) pork sausage
2 tomatoes
2 onions
2 garlic cloves
1/2 bunch flat-leaf parsley
1/2 lb (250g) streaky bacon
1/2 cup (125 ml) dry white wine
8 tbsp olive oil
3/4 cup (100g) pine nuts
1/3 cup (50g) raisins
1-1/2 cups (350ml) meat stock
1 tsp sweet paprika

• Preheat the oven to 360°F (180°C). Break the cabbage into individual leaves and wash.
• Cut out the thick ribs so the leaves lie flat. Blanch the cabbage leaves briefly in salted water; rinse them with cold water and drain. Lay the cabbage leaves individually on the work surface.
• Now, wash the tomatoes and peel the onions and garlic. Chop the onions finely, put the garlic through a press, and wash the parsley; pat dry and chop.
• Cut the pork tenderloin into 12 slices and season with salt and pepper. Heat 2 tbsp olive oil in a frying pan and lightly brown the meat pieces on all sides.
• Cut the sausage into 12 slices. Put a slice of pork together with a slice of sausage and wrap in a cabbage leaf. Place the cabbage rolls tightly together or on top of each other in a fireproof baking dish.

• For the sauce, chop the bacon. Slice the tomatoes across, drop into boiling water, rinse in cold water, peel them, and cut into small cubes.
• Heat the remaining olive oil in a saucepan. Lightly fry the bacon; add the onions, garlic, and tomatoes and braise for 5 minutes. Add the wine and let it boil down a bit. Add the meat stock and raisins and cook for 5 minutes at low heat. Add the pine nuts and parsley to the sauce, season with salt and pepper, and sprinkle with paprika.
• Pour the sauce over the cabbage rolls (they should be covered, so, if needed, fill up the baking dish with some meat stock) and bake in the oven for about 20 minutes.

Smoked Pork Shoulder with Pineapple Glaze

Six Servings
1 can pineapple slices (850ml)
1-1/2 cups (300g) brown sugar
1 cup (250ml) of water
3 tbsp grainy mustard
2 lbs. (1kg) smoked pork shoulder (see page 53)
About 30 cloves
3/4 cup (200ml) dry white wine
1 jar of fruit mustard (as desired)

• Cut the pineapple into small pieces and bring to a boil with their juice, sugar, and some water. Skim off the foam and simmer over low heat for about 60-75 minutes.
• Pour the pineapple compote in a bowl and let cool. • Stir in the mustard and then place, covered, in the refrigerator for three days.
• Preheat the oven to 360°F (180°C). Score the fat on the pork shoulder and insert a clove at each cross.
• Put the pork shoulder in a roasting pan, add wine, and brush the studded surface with the pineapple glaze. Cover with aluminum foil and bake on the lowest rack of the oven for about an hour.
• Remove from the oven and raise the temperature to 425°F (220°C). Brush the pork shoulder with the remaining glaze and put it back into the hot oven, without the foil, for 30 minutes. Remove from the oven and let rest for about 30 minutes before serving. Serve with the jar of fruit mustard.

Seasoned Beef

(Caraway Goulash)

Six Servings
2 onions
1 red bell pepper
3 tbsp lard
2 lbs. (1kg) hot smoked pork shoulder (see page 53)
1 tbsp caraway seeds
1 cup (250ml) beef stock (from a jar)
2 tbsp sweet paprika
1/3 cup (100ml) cream
Black pepper

• Peel the onions and cut into large cubes. Wash the pepper, pat dry, and cut in half. Cut out the seeds and stem, and slice the bell pepper into bite-size pieces.
• Now, cut the mat into chunks, heat the lard, and brown the meat in it briefly. Add the onion and pepper cubes and continue to brown over medium heat for about 5 minutes.
• Sprinkle in the caraway seeds and stir well several times. Pour in half the beef stock, add the paprika, mix well, and cook over a low to medium heat for about an hour. Now, gradually pour in the beef stock. Finally, stir in the cream and add pepper to taste.

Variation: This goes very well with pan-fried potatoes (see page 90) or brown bread.

Bigos

(Polish national dish)

Four Servings

3/4 cup (100g) dried prunes
1/2 cup (125 ml) red wine
1 lb. (500g) white cabbage
1 onion
3 tomatoes
1 clove of garlic
4 sprigs of mint (marjoram)
2 tbsp lard
1 bay leaf
1 lb. (500g) smoked pork shoulder (see page 53)
Black pepper
1/2 lb. (250g) sauerkraut
1/3 ounce (10g) dried porcini mushrooms
1 tbsp flour

• Soak the prunes in lukewarm water.
• Wash the cabbage, cut in half, lay it with the cut surface down on a chopping board, and cut into thin strips.
• Peel the onion and chop.
• Wash the tomatoes; pat dry and dice.

• Wash the mint/marjoram, pat dry, and strip off the leaves; peel the garlic clove and put it through a press.
• Cut the pork shoulder into bite-sized pieces.
• Brown the onions in lard and season with mint/marjoram, bay leaf, garlic, and pepper.
• Add the tomatoes and deglaze with red wine; now, add the meat cubes. Cover and braise on a low heat for about 60 minutes.
• Cook the cabbage in salted water for 20 minutes, rinse, let drain, and add, together with the sauerkraut, to the meat.
• Sprinkle in the dried porcini mushrooms.
• Cut the prunes in half and, if needed, add some water; cover, and cook over low heat for 15 minutes.
• Sprinkle flour over the cabbage and mix everything together well.
• Serve with boiled potatoes or rustic bread.

Smoked Pork Neck with Broad Beans

Six Servings

3 lbs. (1.5kg) cold smoked pork neck (see "cold smoked pork tenderloin," page 53)
1 bunch soup greens (leek, carrot, celery)
2 bay leaves
1 onion, studded with 3 cloves
2 lbs. (1kg) broad beans
4 sprigs lovage
3-1/2 tbsp (50g) butter
1 tbsp flour
1 bay leaf
2 cloves
Savory
Salt
Black pepper

• If the pork neck has become too salty due to brining or smoking, soak it in water for several hours. Put the meat into a large pot with water and bring to a boil.
• Skim off the foam with a spoon.
• Trim and clean the soup greens; chop and add to the meat with the bay leaves and clove-studded onion. Reduce the heat, cover, and let simmer for 1-1/2 hours.
• Hull the broad beans and blanch for 5 minutes in boiling water. Wash the lovage, pat dry, and chop.

• Melt the butter in a saucepan, add flour, and cook smooth while stirring. Remove from heat and let cool slightly, and then add 1 cup (250ml) of hot meat stock and stir well. Simmer for about 10 minutes.
• Season with salt, pepper, and lovage to taste. Add the beans and simmer over low heat for several minutes.

Variation: This dish also goes well with potatoes.

Smoked Pork Loin Roast with Cabbage

Six Servings
3 lbs. (1.5kg) smoked pork loin (see "cold smoked pork tenderloin," page 53)
6 tbsp oil
Salt
1 tsp sugar
4 bay leaves
1 tsp juniper berries
3/4 cup (200ml) veal stock
1 cabbage, about 2 pounds (1kg)
1/4 lb (100g) onions
1 cup (250ml) of dry riesling wine
1/4 cup (50ml) whipping cream
1 cup (200g) crème fraîche
Pepper
1 tsp cornstarch

• Put the smoked pork loin roast in a roasting pan with 4 tbsp hot oil and brown on all sides; add the bay leaves and juniper, and then deglaze with veal stock. Add 3/4 cup (200ml) water. Cook on the lowest rack of a preheated oven at 340°F (170°C) for two hours.

• Cut the cabbage into quarters, cut out the stalk, and slice into long thin strips. Chop the onions finely. Heat the remaining oil in a large pan and sauté the onions and cabbage for 5 minutes, adding just very little salt and sugar. Deglaze with wine and add to the roaster in the oven during the last hour of cooking time.

• Take the roast from the pan, wrap in aluminum foil, and let rest for ten minutes. Boil the cabbage on the stove. Stir in the cream and crème fraîche and boil down for 5 minutes. Beat the cornstarch with a little cold water until smooth and add to the cabbage to thicken. Season with salt, the remaining sugar, pepper, and the remaining Riesling wine to taste.

• Carve the roast into slices. Serve with the cabbage and ready-mix bread dumplings.

Pork Cutlet Skewers with Pineapple Rice

Four Servings

1 cup (200g) long grain rice
3 tbsp maple syrup
1 can of pineapple chunks (580ml)
Sea salt
Black pepper
1 lb. (500g) cold-smoked pork tenderloin (see page 53)
2 red bell peppers
2 spring onions
A walnut-sized piece of ginger
3 tbsp peanut oil
1 lime cut in eighths
Four wooden skewers

• Cook the rice according to instructions and set aside.
• Drain the pineapple, reserving the juice, and mix it with the maple syrup.
• Cut the meat into 3/4" x 3/4" (2x2cm) cubes.
• Wash the peppers, cut in half, and pat dry; remove the seeds and chop the halves into 3/4" x 3/4" (2x2cm) pieces. Wash the spring onions, pat dry, and slice into rings. Peel and grate the ginger.
• Alternate pieces of meat and red pepper on the four skewers. Brush with the syrup [original says honey] and season with salt and pepper.
• Heat 2 tbsp peanut oil in a large frying pan and brown the skewers over medium heat for about 12-15 minutes, turning them several times and constantly brushing them with the maple syrup mixture.
• Mix the rice with the remaining peanut oil, drained pineapple pieces, spring onions, and ginger. Serve on four plates; arrange skewers on top.

Variation: The skewers will taste even heartier if you use smoked beef tenderloin instead of smoked pork.

Smoked Pork Shoulder in Bread Dough Crust

Eight Servings

6 cups. (750g) wheat flour
1-1/2 cubes yeast
1 pinch of sugar
3 tsp salt
2 tbsp caraway seeds
1 tbsp olive oil
2/3 cup (150ml) water
4 lbs. (2kg) hot-smoked pork shoulder (see page 53)
1 onion
2 bay leaves
10 juniper berries
10 cloves
Oil for the baking pan

• Dissolve the yeast in 1/4 cup (50ml) of luke-warm water and the sugar. Put the flour into a bowl, make a small hole in the middle, and pour in the dissolved yeast. Stir slightly and leave covered for 2 minutes.

• Add the salt, caraway, the remaining water, and olive oil and then knead into a smooth dough. Let rise for about 3 hours in a warm, dark place.

• Bring two 2 quarts of water to a boil, with the whole peeled onion, bay leaves, juniper berries, and cloves. Add the pork shoulder and let it simmer for about an hour; now, take out the stock, drain well, and let cool.

• Roll out the dough and wrap the pork shoulder in it, tucking the edges of the dough under the meat. Make a couple of cuts in the top of the dough and let stand another 20 minutes.

• Preheat the oven to 390°F (200°C). Place the pork shoulder on a greased baking sheet and bake for 60-75 minutes. Serve with mustard fruits from the jar or sauerkraut.

Fettuccine Alfredo with Smoked Pork Tenderloin

Four Servings

7 ounces (200g) button mushrooms
2 shallots
1 clove of garlic
2 cups (300g) frozen peas
1 lb. (500g) fettuccine
Salt
1 lb (500g) cold-smoked pork tenderloin (see page 53)
3 tbsp clarified butter
2 sprigs of savory
Black pepper
3/4 cup (200ml) whipping cream
Freshly grated Parmesan cheese

• Clean the mushrooms using paper towels, trim the stems, and cut into thin slices. Peel the shallots and chop finely. Peel the garlic and press. Cook the pasta and the peas separately in salted water, according to the package instructions.

• Carve the pork tenderloin into thin slices and then melt the butter in a pan. Sauté the mushrooms and onion about 5 minutes; remove and set aside. Drain the pasta and peas.

• In the remaining fat, brown the pork briefly and then add the mushroom-onion mixture, the peas, and the savory. Mix everything well and season with pepper. Pour in the cream and bring to a boil briefly.

• Pour the pasta into a warmed bowl and toss with the sauce. Serve with freshly grated Parmesan cheese.

Variation: This dish also works well with smoked beef or venison fillet (see pages 54 and 56).

Smoked Pork Neck Steaks on Apples and Leeks

Four Servings
1 lb. (500g) leeks
4 apples (such as Jonathan, russet)
3 tbsp (40g) butter
3/4 cup (200ml) hard cider
2/3 cup (60g) crème fraîche
1 tsp grainy mustard
Salt
White pepper
4 freshly smoked pork neck steaks, 5-6 oz./150-180g (see page 52)

• Clean the leeks, cut in half lengthwise, wash, and cut into narrow strips. Wash the apples, pat dry, cut in quarters; core and dice them.
• Heat the butter in a large frying pan; add the leeks and sauté for 5 minutes while stirring. Add the apples and cook briefly. Deglaze with hard cider and let simmer about 10 minutes.
• Mix the crème fraîche with the mustard and fold into the leek-apple mixture, and season with salt and pepper.
• Arrange the freshly smoked pork neck steaks with the leek-apple mixture on four plates and serve.

Pearl Barley Soup with Smoked Pork Shoulder

Four Servings
3 tbsp sunflower oil
1/2 lb (250g) each of carrots, leeks, celery root, and onions
2 potatoes
7 ounces (200g) pearl barley
1 lb (500g) smoked pork shoulder (see page 53)
2 quarts (2 liters) beef stock (from a cube)
1 bay leaf
1 bunch lovage

• Peel the carrots and celery root and chop into small cubes. Peel the onions and chop. Trim the leeks, cut lengthwise, and wash; cut into thin strips. Wash the lovage, pat dry, and chop.
• Heat the oil in a saucepan and sweat the diced vegetables in it. Pour in the beef stock and gradually add the pearl barley. Add the meat and bring to a boil briefly. Add the bay leaf and lovage to the stock and let simmer at a low heat for about an hour.

Variation: The soup also works well with smoked Oxtail (see page 89).

Smoked Pork Cutlets
with Broccoli

Four Servings
1 lb (500g) broccoli
1 tbsp olive oil
4 smoked pork cutlets, about 7 ounces/200g
(see page 52)
4-1/2 tbsp (60g) butter
Pine nuts
4 slices serrano ham
Salt
Black pepper
Grated nutmeg
3/4 cup (200ml) meat stock
1 sprig of thyme
1 tsp dijon mustard

• Wash the broccoli, cut into florets, and cook until al dente.
• Heat the oil in the pan and brown the cutlets on each side; take out and keep warm.
• Melt the butter in the pan until it foams lightly. Reduce heat, and add the broccoli, pine nuts, and finely chopped ham. Add salt and pepper and season with nutmeg.
• Rinse the thyme sprig, pat dry, and strip off the leaves. Heat the stock with the mustard and add the thyme leaves.
• Arrange the broccoli and cutlets on four plates and pour sauce over the meat. This dish goes well with pan-fried potatoes (see page 90).

Smoked Lamb Chops
with Kidney Beans

Four Servings
1 bunch of parsley
2 sprigs thyme
2 garlic cloves
1 beefsteak tomato
6 tbsp olive oil
1/2 tsp lemon pepper
8 smoked lamb chops
(see "hot smoked lamb fillets," page 55)
Black pepper
2 jars of kidney beans, 15 ounces (425g)

• Wash the parsley and thyme and pat dry. Chop the parsley and strip the thyme leaves from the stalks. Peel and press the garlic.
• Mix 4 tbsp olive oil with the lemon pepper and thyme and rub into the lamb chops. Heat the remaining olive oil and brown the lamb chops briefly on both sides, and then remove and keep warm.
• Cube the beefsteak tomato, add to the hot pan with the garlic, and sauté briefly. Drain the beans and add.
• Heat briefly and arrange with two lamb chops each on four plates. These go well with pan-fried potatoes (see page 90).

Smoked Leg of Lamb with Pepper Sauce and Fried Polenta

Six Servings
4 bell peppers
7 ounces (200g) onions
2 garlic cloves
8 tbsp olive oil
2 cups (500ml) lamb stock (from a jar)
3/4 cup (200ml) whipping cream
Lemon pepper
Salt
1/2 lb. (250g) polenta (Italian cornmeal)
1 tsp salt
1 tbsp butter
1 cup (100g) of grated Parmesan
1 freshly smoked leg of lamb

• Prepare the cornmeal the day before as follows: Bring 1 quart/liter of water to a boil, add salt, and stir in the cornmeal. Let thicken over low heat for 20 minutes. Stir.
• Stir in the butter and mix well with Parmesan cheese.
• Pour the cornmeal into a loaf pan and let cool.
• Cut the peppers in half lengthwise and remove the seeds. With the skin side up, lay on a baking sheet. Put under the pre-heated oven grill on the second rack from the top and grill until the skin forms black bubbles.
• Remove from the oven, cover with a damp kitchen towel, and cool for 30 minutes. Now, remove the skin and cut the peppers into large pieces. Chop the onions and garlic into small cubes.

• Heat 4 tbsp olive oil; add onions and garlic and cook until translucent. Add the peppers and sauté briefly together. Fill the pan with lamb stock and cook for 10 minutes over medium heat. Pour in the cream and let simmer for another 10 minutes. Puree very smooth using a hand-held blender. Let come to a boil briefly and season with lemon pepper and salt to taste; set aside.
• Cut the cornmeal into 3/4" (2cm) thick slices. Heat 4 tbsp oil in a pan and fry the slices over medium heat on both sides until brown.
• If necessary, warm up the lamb leg in the oven. Carve the meat into slices and arrange with the cornmeal and pepper sauce on six plates.

Stew with
Smoked Ox Leg

Four Servings
1 bunch soup greens
1 large onion
10 juniper berries
4 tbsp oil
2 slices fresh smoked ox leg, 3/4 lb/350g (see "hot smoked pork chops," page 52)
2 bay leaves
12 black peppercorns
1 lb (400g) carrots
3/4 cup (100g) dried prunes
10-1/2 ounces (300g) potatoes
1 bunch of parsley

• Wash the soup greens, trim, and chop coarsely into pieces. Halve the onion and put in a pan with the cut surface down. Fry at medium to high heat until the cut surfaces turn dark brown.
• Crush the juniper berries. Heat the oil in a roasting pan, pat the meat dry, and sear over medium heat for 2 minutes on each side; remove. Fry the soup greens in the pan drippings briefly.
• Add onion, juniper berries, bay leaves, peppercorns, and 2 quarts/liters of water, and bring to a boil; cover. Add the ox leg slices and simmer over low heat for 1-1/2 hours in the half-covered pan.
• Wash the carrots and potatoes; peel and cut into cubes.

• Take the meat out of the stock and pour the stock through a sieve into a saucepan; bring to a boil. Halve the prunes and add to the stock with the carrots and potatoes; cover and cook over low heat for 20 minutes.
• Wash the parsley, pat dry, and chop.
• Cut the meat from the bone in large pieces and return to the stock. Divide the stew among four plates and serve garnished with parsley.

Variation: Instead of ox leg, you can also make this soup with 1-1/2 pounds (750g) smoked pork shoulder (see page 53).

Smoked Beef Billet with Homemade Herb Butter and Pan-fried Potatoes

Four Servings
1 lb. (500-600g) waxy potatoes
Salt
2 tbsp (100g) butter, softened
1 bunch of mixed herbs (tarragon, dill, chervil, parsley)
1 tsp lemon pepper
1 onion
1/4 cup (50g) clarified butter
Black pepper
4 freshly smoked beef fillets, 5 oz./150g (see page 54)

• The day before wash and peel the potatoes, and then cook in salted water for 25 minutes. After cooling, cover with wrap and put in a cool place.
• Beat the butter with an electric mixer until creamy white. Finely chop the herbs; season the butter with the herbs, lemon zest, salt, and pepper. Cover and chill for 30 minutes. Slice the potatoes. Melt the clarified butter in a large frying pan and sauté the onions. Add the potatoes and fry at medium heat for 15 minutes, turning often, until golden brown. Add salt and pepper.
• Arrange the freshly smoked fillets on four plates and serve the herb butter and the fried potatoes. This goes well with a mixed salad.

Smoked Lamb Fillet with Figs in Port Wine

Six Servings
1 cup (250ml) port wine
1/3 cup (100ml) light red wine
1 tbsp brown sugar
3 cloves
2 allspice berries
1 bay leaf
6 ripe figs
1 sprig of rosemary
6 freshly smoked fillets of lamb (see page 55)
Black pepper
Sea salt
2 tbsp olive oil

• Bring the port wine to a boil with the red wine, sugar, cloves, allspice berries, and bay leaf. Prick the figs with a fork several times, cut off the tips, and cook lightly for 3 minutes in the port-wine liquor; let the figs cool in it.
• Wash the rosemary sprig, pat dry, tear off the needles, and chop coarsely. Take the figs out of the liquor, and cut each into four wedges. Pour the liquor through a sieve and simmer until syrupy. Arrange the fig wedges on four plates.
• Put the fillets in a pan with melted butter and fry briefly, each cut diagonally into three pieces, and arrange on the figs. Drizzle with fig liquor and garnish with rosemary. Serve with a fresh baguette.

Poached Smoked Beef Fillet with Steamed Carrots

Four Servings
1-2/3 cups (400ml) vegetable or beef stock (from a jar)
1 lb. (500-600g) beef fillet
1 lb. (500-600g) carrots
4 tbsp butter
1-1/2 bunch flat-leaf parsley
2 stalks dill
1/2 bunch tarragon
2 shallots
1-1/2 tbsp (20g) butter
3 tbsp white wine
1 cup (250ml) whipping cream
Pepper
Sugar
Kitchen string

• Bring the stock and about 1-1/2 quarts/liters of water to a boil. Tie the tenderloin with kitchen string and fasten to a wooden spoon. Hang the meat into the pot of stock, so that it can float freely and cook evenly. Poach over low heat for 15 minutes. Remove the meat and smoke for 20 minutes in a wok over hickory sawdust and herbs to taste (see page 27).

• Wash and pat dry the carrots, and then slice thinly. Melt the butter in a pan, pour in 3/4 cup (200ml) of water, add salt, and bring to a boil. Add the carrots to the pot and steam for 10 minutes over low heat.

• Wash 1/2 bunch of parsley, pat dry, and chop. Sprinkle over the finished steamed carrots.

• Remove the remaining parsley and other herbs from their stems and chop.

• Peel and dice the shallots.

• Melt the butter over low heat and sauté the diced shallots. Stir in the white wine, add cream, and boil down till creamy. Season with salt, pepper, and a pinch of sugar and take off the heat.

• Add the chopped herbs and 6 tbsp of the beef stock to the sauce and taste; don't allow it to boil any more. Divide the sauce on four plates. Cut the tenderloin into four slices (remove the kitchen string) and put each slice on the sauce. Serve with carrots and pan-fried potatoes (see page 90).

Smoked Oxtail Ragout

Six Servings
2 onions
4 carrots
12 ounces (350g) celery
1 small celery
1/4 lb (100g) streaky, smoked bacon
5 garlic cloves
3 lbs. (1-1/2kg) smoked oxtail in 1" to 1-1/2" thick
(3-4cm) slices (see "Hot Smoked Pork Chops,"
page 52)
Some flour
Pepper
9 tbsp olive oil
1 can tomatoes (50ml)
1 tube tomato paste
3/4 cup (100g) raisins
3/4 cup (100g) pine nuts
1 bunch basil
1/2 tsp each of thyme, oregano, marjoram
2 bay leaves
1/2 quart/liter dry red wine
1/2 quart/liter beef stock

• Peel and dice the onions, carrots, and celery.
Clean the celery, trim the ends, and cut the stalks
into thin slices. Press the garlic and dice the bacon.
• Mix the flour with the pepper and coat the oxtail
pieces with it. Now, heat 3 tbsp olive oil in a large
frying pan and brown the oxtail pieces on all sides.
• Sauté the onions, bacon, and garlic in the remaining olive oil and then add the oxtail pieces.

• Add the vegetables and herbs to the pan, cook
about 4 minutes; deglaze with 1/3 cup (100ml)
of wine.
• Stir in the tomato paste and pour the beef stock
over the meat. Add the raisins and pine nuts, and
season with pepper. Bring to a simmer over low
heat, occasionally stirring, and then simmer for
1-1/2 hours. Keep topping up alternately with
wine and stock.
• Serve with grilled polenta (see page 88).

Smoked Beef Brisket
with Oven-baked Beans

Eight Servings
1-1/2 lbs. (750g) dried white beans
3 tbsp brown sugar
2 tsp salt
Salt, black pepper
2 tbsp dijon mustard
2 tbsp sugar beet syrup
1/3 cup (100ml) ketchup
2/3 cup (150ml) maple syrup
2 thick slices of smoked streaky bacon
4-2/5 lbs. (2kg) fresh smoked beef brisket
(see page 54)

• Put the beans in a pot and cover with lightly salted water; simmer for one hour. Preheat the oven to 300°F (150°C).
• Put the sugar, salt, pepper, mustard, sugar beet syrup, ketchup, and maple syrup in a large bowl and stir. Drain the beans and add.
• Put one slice of bacon on the bottom of an oven-proof dish or cast-iron pot. Pour in the beans and lay the second slice of bacon on top. Cover the beans with boiling water; if using a baking dish, cover with aluminum foil, or if a pot, put on the lid.
• Let cook for 5 hours; meanwhile, keep topping up with some water. During the last half hour, take off the foil or the lid.
• Serve the beans with "smoked brisket Texas style."

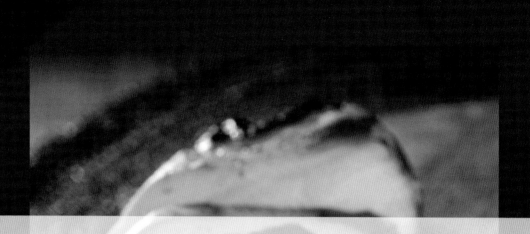

Poultry

Gratin of Smoked
Turkey Cutlet

Four Servings
1 bunch arugula
1/4 cup (30g) pine nuts
1/2 cup (50g) grated pecorino
1/4 cup (30g) grated gouda
1/2 lb. (250g) small vine-ripened tomatoes
1 medium onion
4 tbsp olive oil
8 small smoked turkey cutlets (see "Hot Smoked Chicken Breast," page 57)
Salt
5 ounces (150ml) dry white vermouth (Noilly Prat®)
1 pinch of sugar
1/4 cup (50ml) whipping cream

• Wash and pat dry the arugula and cut into narrow strips. Chop the pine nuts. Mix the grated cheese with the argula and pine nuts.
• Wash the tomatoes, quarter them, and pat dry. Peel and chop onions.
• Heat oil in a pan; sauté the onions and cherry tomatoes for a minute in the pan and deglaze with vermouth. Add the sugar and cream and bring to a boil.
• Put the freshly smoked turkey cutlets in a shallow, flame-proof dish, spread the cheese mixture on top, and grill in the oven for about 4 minutes.
• Serve topped with the sauce.

Smoked Goose Breast
with Champagne Sauerkraut

Four Servings
2 tbsp goose fat
5-1/4 cups (750g) fresh sauerkraut
2 juniper berries
1 bay leaf
1 cup (250ml) champagne (or sparkling wine)
20 green seedless grapes
1 hot smoked goose breast (see "Hot Smoked Turkey Legs," page 57)

• Heat the goose fat in a saucepan and cook the sauerkraut briefly, along with the spices. Gradually add the champagne and simmer about 15 minutes.
• Wash the grapes and cut in half; quarter any larger grapes.
• Cut the freshly smoked goose breast into slices.
• Remove the sauerkraut from the heat and mix the grapes in well. Arrange the goose breast and sauerkraut on a platter and serve.

Variation: This dish also goes well with bread dumplings.

Smoked Goose Liver on Savoy Cabbage with Pomegranate Seeds

Four Servings
1/2 cup (100g) cane sugar
1/3 cup (100g) coarse sea salt
1 tsp mixed peppercorns from the mill
4 goose livers, about 1/4 lb (130g)
per piece
2 shallots
1 lb. (500-600g) savoy cabbage
4 tbsp butter
1/4 cup (50ml) port wine
3 ounces (100ml) chicken stock
1 pomegranate

• Mix the cane sugar, salt, and pepper. Sprinkle over the goose livers so that they are completely covered, and let marinate about 30 minutes.
• Rub off the marinade and pat the goose livers dry. Let them dry for about an hour in a cool, airy place, and then smoke the goose livers for about 5 minutes in a wok (see "Hot Smoked Duck Breast," page 57).
• Peel the shallots and cut into small cubes. Cut out the cabbage stalk, remove the outer leaves, and cut the cabbage into inch-wide strips. Bring salted water to a boil; blanch the cabbage in it for 2 minutes and pour the water off. Rinse with cold water and drain well.
• Heat the butter in a frying pan, add the diced shallots, and sauté until translucent; sprinkle on the sugar and caramelize. Deglaze with port wine and chicken stock and let boil down a bit. Add the cabbage and cook for another 2 minutes. Season with salt, pepper, and nutmeg.
• Put the cabbage on four plates and arrange the goose liver on top. Halve the pomegranate and garnish the goose liver with the seeds. Serve with toast.

Smoked Duck Breast on Lentil and Orange Salad

Four Servings
1-1/3 cup (100g) puy lentils
2-1/2 cups (50g) lamb's lettuce
2 oranges, 1 untreated
1 red onion
1 clove of garlic
4 tbsp orange juice
4 tbsp olive oil
Sea salt
Black pepper from the mill
1 tsp ground cumin
1/2 tsp brown sugar
Chili powder
2 large, freshly smoked duck breasts,
approximately 10-1/2 ounces/300g (see page 57)

• Put the lentils in a saucepan and cover with water; cook for 30 minutes. Pour off the water, drain well, and let cool slightly.
• Wash the lamb's lettuce and drain.
• Grate the zest from the untreated orange and set aside. Peel the rest of the grated orange and peel the other orange completely; also remove the white pith. Cut out the segments of both oranges and put in a bowl.
• Peel the onion, cut in half, slice into thin rings, and mix with the oranges. Peel and press the garlic. Mix the olive oil and orange juice with the grated orange zest, and season with salt, pepper, cumin, sugar, and chili powder to taste.
• Carefully fold the lamb's lettuce and lentils into the orange-onion mixture. Pour on the salad dressing and serve with freshly smoked and sliced duck.

Bean Stew with
Smoked Chicken Legs

Four Servings
1/2 lb (200g) onions
2 garlic cloves
1 sprig rosemary
4 sprigs thyme
8 smoked chicken legs (see page 57)
6 tbsp olive oil
Salt, black pepper
5 ounces (150ml) dry red wine
5 ounces (150ml) chicken stock (from a jar)
14 ounces (400g) peeled canned tomatoes (850g)
1 jar of white beans (15oz/425g)
1 can red kidney beans (15oz/425g)
1 zucchini
1 red bell pepper
1 yellow bell pepper
1 fresh red chili

• Peel the onions and chop coarsely. Peel and press the garlic cloves. Chop the herbs and pat dry. Strip off the rosemary and thyme leaves and chop finely. Heat 3 tbsp of olive oil and brown the chicken legs on all sides. Remove and set aside.
• Preheat the oven to 390°F (200°C).
• Sauté the onions and garlic in 1 tbsp olive oil until translucent and add half the herbs. Season with salt and pepper and deglaze with red wine and chicken stock. Add the white and red beans and tomatoes with their juice, and cook all together on the bottom rack for 25 minutes.
• Trim and wash the zucchini, and cut into half-inch thick slices. Halve the peppers, remove the cores, peel with a vegetable peeler, and cut into bite-size pieces. Halve the chili pepper; remove veins and core and chop finely. Heat the remaining olive oil and sauté the zucchini at a high heat until golden brown.

• Add the remaining herbs to the peppers and chili. Season with salt and pepper. Add the chicken legs, and continue to cook for 10 minutes in the oven. Serve in soup bowls with a baguette.

Variation: You can also prepare this bean stew with smoked wild boar (see page 16).

Smoked Chicken Pie

4 servings
3 pieces of frozen puff pastry
1 carrot
1 onion
1 fennel bulb
2 tbsp butter
1/2 cup (50g) flour
1 cup (250ml) milk
1-3/4 cups (400ml) chicken stock (from a jar)
Lemon pepper
Juice of 1/2 lemon
1 smoked chicken, 2 lbs./1,000g (see page 56)
Flour for rolling

• Thaw the puff pastry. Peel the carrot and onion and chop into small cubes. Trim and wash the fennel; cut into cubes.
• Preheat oven to 390°F (200°C).
• Heat the butter in a saucepan and sauté the vegetables for 8-10 minutes. Sprinkle in the flour and stir for about 2 minutes. Gradually pour in the milk and chicken stock and stir until you have a smooth, white sauce. Season with lemon pepper and lemon juice to taste. Simmer for 6-8 minutes, stirring constantly.
• Take the chicken meat off the bone, cut into bite-sized pieces, add to the sauce, and pour the mixture into an ovenproof dish.
• Lay out the thawed puff pastry sheets and, depending on the size of the ovenproof dish, roll out on a floured work surface either into a round or oval shape. Brush the lower edge of the dough with beaten egg yolk, lay the dough over the filled dish, and crimp the overhanging edges.
• Bake for 20-25 minutes in the oven and let cool slightly before serving.

Potato Gratin with Smoked Duck Breast

Four Servings
1 pound (500-600g) waxy potatoes
1 tbsp butter
1 cup (250ml) cream
Salt, nutmeg
7 ounces (200g) gouda or edam cheese
1 freshly smoked duck breast, about 12oz/350g (see page 57)

• Preheat the oven to 360°F (180°C).
• Wash the potatoes, peel, and slice thinly. Butter an ovenproof dish and place the potato slices in layers.
• Season the cream with salt and nutmeg and pour over the potato slices. Grate the cheese coarsely and sprinkle on the potatoes. Bake in the oven about 45 minutes.
• Slice the duck breast into 1/2-inch thick pieces.
• After the gratin has baked for 25 minutes, arrange the duck breast on the cheese and continue to bake another 20 minutes. Serve with mixed salad.

Party Platter:
Smoked Chicken Legs
and Smoked Bratwurst
on Potato Salad

Four Servings

2 lbs. (1kg) waxy potatoes
Salt
1/4 quart/liter of beef stock (from a cube)
1 onion
1 tart apple
3 gherkins (cucumbers)
1 bunch of parsley
1 cup (200g) mayonnaise
1/2 cup (100g) yogurt
White pepper, salt
8 freshly smoked chicken legs (see page 57)
8 freshly smoked bratwurst (the sausages are not cured, but smoked with the chicken legs)

• The day before, cook the potatoes in salted water, peel, and put in a bowl; cover with saran wrap and put in a cool place. When the potatoes are cool, slice thinly and put in a salad bowl. Pour over the hot beef bouillon and set aside.
• Peel the onion; cut into small cubes and add to the potatoes. Wash the apple and pat dry, and then quarter and core it. Cut the cucumbers and apple quarters into small cubes and set aside.

• Wash the parsley, pat dry, and chop. Mix the mayonnaise with the yogurt and season with salt and white pepper.
• Fold the mayonnaise mixture into the potatoes, mix in the apple and cucumber pieces, and let stand for about 2 hours.
• Serve the potato salad with the freshly smoked chicken legs and bratwurst.

Variation: Instead of an apple, you can also use two seeded, diced tomatoes in the salad.

Smoked Chicken Breast with Couscous Salad

Four Servings
4 smoked chicken breasts (see page 57)
1-1/5" (3cm) piece of fresh ginger
2 shallots
1 clove of garlic
2 ounces (50g) sultanas
Salt
1-1/4 cup (200g) couscous (instant)
8 tbsp olive oil
4 tbsp lemon juice
3 ounces (100ml) chicken stock (from a jar)
1/2 cup (60g) pine nuts
Pepper
Chili pepper
1/2 tsp cinnamon

• Peel the ginger and chop into very small cubes.
• Peel the shallots and garlic, and also chop finely.
• Bring 1 cup (250ml) of salted water to a boil and pour over the couscous; stir and let stand for 5 minutes, and then loosen the couscous grains with a fork.
• Toast the pine nuts in an uncoated pan until golden brown and let cool. Heat the olive oil and sauté the ginger, shallots, and garlic in it. Deglaze with chicken stock and lemon and add to the still-warm couscous. Season with salt, pepper, chili pepper, and cinnamon to taste.
• Mix in the pine nuts and raisins and let the couscous salad stand for about 30 minutes. Serve with the freshly smoked chicken breasts.

Smoked Turkey Legs with Mixed Salad

Four Servings
2 brined turkey legs (see page 57)
2 sprigs of sage
Lemon pepper
1 iceberg lettuce
1/2 small red cabbage
1 large carrot
4 stalks celery
1 shallot
1 tbsp corn oil
4 tbsp apple cider vinegar
2 tbsp vegetable stock
Salt
Black pepper
1 apple
4 tbsp chopped walnuts

• Slice the brined and dried turkey legs lengthwise and remove the bone with a sharp, pointed knife. Lay the meat flat on a work surface and sprinkle with lemon pepper. Put a sage stalk in the middle. Roll up the turkey legs, tie with kitchen string, and smoke as described on page 57.
• Wash the lettuce and red cabbage and slice into thin strips. Wash the carrot, pat dry, peel, and grate coarsely. Clean, wash, and pat dry the celery stalks and cut into thin slices. Put everything in a large bowl.
• Make vinaigrette of the oil, vinegar, vegetable stock, salt, and pepper and toss with the salad.
• Wash the apple, cut into quarters, core, and chop into small cubes and, with the walnuts, sprinkle over the salad.
• Carve the turkey leg into 3/4" (2cm) thick slices, arrange on four plates, and serve with the salad.

Game

Smoked Saddle of Hare with Cranberry Sauce

Four Servings
4 apples (Jonagold)
1-1/4 cup (150g) dried cranberries
1 clove
10 ounces (300ml) water
Juice of 1/2 lemon
1 cinnamon stick
1 sprig of rosemary
1 freshly smoked saddle of hare (see page 56)

• Wash, dry, and peel apples, and then quarter and core them and cut into small cubes.
• Put the apples, cranberries, and clove in a pot. Pour in water and lemon juice and bring to a boil. Add the cinnamon stick and rosemary. Simmer over low heat for about 30 minutes, and remove the cinnamon and rosemary.
• Carve the saddle of hare into thin slices and arrange around the cranberry compote. This goes well with hash browns/potatoes (see page 107).

Variation: Instead of cranberries, you can also use 5 ounces (150g) of prepared cranberry jelly.

Smoked Venison Fillets with Brussels Sprout Salad

Four Servings
10-1/2 ounces (300g) Brussels sprouts
Salt
1 shallot
10 walnut meats
1 tsp cane sugar
2 tbsp sherry vinegar
2 tbsp walnut oil
2 tbsp vegetable stock
Black pepper
2 tbsp sultanas
4 freshly smoked venison fillet steaks (see page 56)

• Wash the Brussels sprouts, drain, and remove the outer leaves. Halve the sprouts and blanch for 1-2 minutes in boiling salted water. Pour off the water, rinse with cold water, and drain.
• Peel the shallot and chop finely. Coarsely chop the walnuts and toast in an uncoated pan. Sprinkle with cane sugar and let the nuts caramelize as you keep shaking the pan; allow to cool.
• Mix the vinegar, oil, vegetable stock, and shallot and season with salt and pepper. Now, toss the vinaigrette with the sprout leaves and hearts. Add the raisins and walnuts and serve with the freshly smoked venison steaks.

Variation: Brussels sprout salad also goes well with saddle of venison steaks (see page 107).

Smoked Roast Wild Boar with Blackberry Sauce, Parsnip Puree, and Brussels Sprouts

Eight Servings

1-3/4 lbs. (800g) parsnips
Salt
2 lbs. (1kg) Brussels sprouts
7 ounces (200g) bacon
1 tbsp butter
Pepper
Nutmeg
Mace
1 cup (250ml) cream
1 dash lemon juice
2 shallots
2 tbsp olive oil
1 pound (500-600g) frozen blackberries
8 ounces (200ml) red wine
Salt
Red pepper
1/4 cup (50ml) dark balsamic vinegar
A hot smoked wild boar roast from the leg, approximately 4 lbs./2kg (see "Hot Smoked Pork Shoulder," page 53, but note the brining time for game on page 37)

• Wash and peel the parsnips and pat dry. Cut into cubes, put in a pot, and cover with water. Add salt and cook for 15-20 minutes until soft.
• Clean the Brussels sprouts and make cross cuts into the stalks. Cook in salted water for 15 minutes.
• Cut the bacon into strips and sauté in hot butter in a frying pan. Lower the heat and add the Brussels sprouts. Season with pepper and a little nutmeg. Cover and keep warm.

• Mash the softened cooked parsnips with a fork and season with salt, pepper, and mace. Whip the cream until stiff and fold into the puree. Season with fresh pepper and a squeeze of lemon juice to taste. Cover and keep warm.
• Peel the shallots and dice finely; heat the olive oil and sauté the shallots until translucent. Add the frozen blackberries, pour in the red wine, season with salt and red pepper, and let simmer for 20 minutes.
• Pour on the balsamic vinegar and again briefly bring to a boil.
• Serve the freshly smoked wild boar roast with the parsnip puree, Brussels sprouts with bacon, and blackberry sauce.

Variation: These side dishes also go well with saddle of hare and venison fillet steaks (see page 105).

Smoked Saddle of Venison Steaks with Red Cabbage and Hash Browns

Four Servings
1 tbsp lard
1 jar red cabbage (1 pint/580ml)
1 cinnamon stick
2 cloves
1 glass of red wine
1/4 lb (100g) dried cranberries
Salt
1 pinch of sugar
4 medium floury potatoes
Pepper
Olive oil
4 freshly smoked saddle of venison steaks of 5 ounces/150g (see page 56)

• Heat the lard in a saucepan, add the red cabbage, cinnamon, cloves, and red wine and braise for about 15 minutes. If needed, add some water. During the last 5 minutes, add the cranberries. Mix well. Season the prepared red cabbage with salt and sugar to taste and keep warm.
• Wash the potatoes, peel, and grate coarsely; season with salt and pepper. Heat the oil and shape the grated potatoes into eight small potato cakes; fry as hash browns.
• Arrange the saddle of venison steaks with the red cabbage and hash browns on four plates and serve.

Tofu, Cheese, Eggs & Co.

Vegetable Soup with Smoked Tofu

Four Servings
1 onion
2 potatoes
6 parsley roots
3 carrots
4 celery stalks
3 small garlic cloves
1 leek
3 tbsp olive oil
Salt
1 tsp sugar
1-1/2 quarts/liters vegetable stock
1 pound (500-600g) spinach
Salt
2-1/2 cups (100g) soup noodles
3 tbsp olive oil
3/4 cup (80g) green beans
1/2 pound (250g) smoked tofu
1 red chili pepper

• Peel the onion and potatoes and chop coarsely. Wash the parsley roots and carrots, peel, and chop coarsely. Trim the celery, and then peel and slice. Peel the garlic and press it. Trim the leek, halve it lengthwise, and cut into strips.
• Heat the oil in a pan, add onions and garlic, and sauté over medium heat until translucent.
• Add potatoes, parsley roots, carrots, celery, and leek, and sweat over mild heat for 5 minutes until soft. Season with salt and sugar, pour on the vegetable stock, cover, and cook about 30 minutes.
• Trim the spinach leaves, cut out the thick stems, and wash thoroughly. Blanch the spinach in boiling, salted water for ten seconds, pour into a sieve, and rinse in cold water and drain well. Squeeze out remaining water from the spinach and chop finely.

• Cook the pasta in salted water according to package directions until somewhat firm, pour into a colander, and drain; drizzle over 1 tbsp oil and mix.
• Cut the green beans crosswise into strips; blanch in boiling water for 2 minutes and drain.
• Chop the smoked tofu into 3/8" thick (1cm) cubes. Trim the chili pepper, halve lengthwise, remove the seeds, and dice finely. Heat the remaining oil in a pan; add the green beans and tofu. Sauté over medium heat for 2 minutes and season lightly with salt.
• Add the noodles and spinach to the soup and bring to a boil.
• Ladle the soup into hot bowls, and then add the green bean-tofu mixture and serve immediately. This goes well with toasted baguette slices.

Peppers Stuffed with Smoked Ricotta

Four Servings
1 bunch oregano
2 onions
2 garlic cloves
4 tbsp olive oil
1 pound (500-600g) ground meat
1 tbsp tomato paste
1 cup (250ml) chicken stock (from a cube)
1 can of peeled tomatoes (15 ounces/425g)
Salt
Black pepper
1 pinch of sugar
1 bay leaf
4 green peppers
1/4 cup (50g) cubed toasting bread
5 tbsp olive oil
1/2 cup (100g) smoked ricotta
1 pound (500-600g) ricotta
1 egg
1 egg yolk
Salt
White pepper
1 bunch parsley

• Wash and pat dry the oregano, strip off the leaves, and chop coarsely. Peel the onion and finely chop. Peel and press the garlic.
• Heat the oil in a frying pan and brown the chopped meat well for 5 minutes. Add the onions, garlic, and half the oregano, and cook together for 10 minutes.
• Stir in the tomato paste, deglaze with the stock, and let boil down. Add the tomatoes with their juice to the meat. Season with salt and pepper; add a pinch of sugar and the bay leaf. Add 1 cup (250ml) of water and simmer down for an hour.

• Meanwhile, cut a lid out of the peppers on the stem end and remove the cores with a small knife.
• Cut the bread into small cubes and fry in a pan with 3 tbsp oil until crisp. Finely grate the smoked ricotta and wrap the fresh ricotta in a cloth and lightly squeeze out the liquid. Mix the cheese, egg and egg yolk, the remaining oregano, and bread cubes, and add salt and pepper.
• Fill the peppers with the mixture and set on the lids.
• Pour the sauce into an ovenproof dish, set the peppers in it, and drizzle on the rest of the oil.
• Bake on the lowest rack of a preheated oven at 360°F (180°C) for 40 minutes.
• Wash the parsley, pat dry, and chop.
• Serve the peppers with sauce, garnished with the parsley.

Spinach Casserole with Ham and Smoked Gouda

Four Servings
1-1/2 lbs. (750g) spinach
4 tbsp butter
Salt
White pepper
Nutmeg
6-8 slices of brown bread
6 tbsp olive oil
1/2 lb. (250g) cooked ham, 1/10" thick (2-3mm) slices
7 ounces (200g) smoked gouda (see page 59)

• Preheat oven to 390°F (200°C).
• Sort the spinach, wash carefully, and drain. Melt 2 tbsp butter in a large pot and add the spinach. Cook for 2-3 minutes, stirring occasionally, to wilt the spinach.
• Oil a rectangular baking dish with the olive oil, spread the brown bread slices on the bottom, and put the ham on top.
• Squeeze any remaining liquid from the spinach and spread on the ham; season with salt, pepper, and nutmeg and top with flakes of the remaining butter.
• Coarsely grate the smoked gouda and sprinkle over the spinach. Bake the casserole for 15-20 minutes in the oven.

Calzone with Fennel Salami and Smoked Mozzarella

Four Servings
3 cups (360g) flour
1 envelope of dry yeast
7 tbsp olive oil
Salt
2 red bell peppers
1 fennel bulb, about 5 ounces (150g)
2 ounces (50g) onions
2 garlic cloves
1 ounce (30g) dried tomatoes
1 ounce (30g) pitted black olives
3/4 lb (350g) fennel salami
1 tsp lemon pepper
1/2 lb. (250g) smoked mozzarella (see page 59)
1 ounce (30g) grated Parmesan cheese
Some flour for the work surface

For the dough:
• Combine and knead the flour, yeast with 2 tbsp olive oil, 1 cup (225ml) of lukewarm water, and some salt into a smooth dough; cover and put in a warm place for 2 hours to rise. Knead the dough once again and let stand for an additional hour to rise.
• Wash and cut in half the peppers, core them, and place with the skin side up on a baking sheet. Roast them on the upper rack under the oven grill for 6-8 minutes until black bubbles form. Cover the pepper halves with a damp kitchen towel for 10 minutes, and then peel and dice into 3/8" (1cm) pieces.
• Trim the fennel and dice very finely; do the same with the onions, garlic, and tomatoes. Chop the olives very small.

• Put all the ingredients in a large pot with 4 tbsp olive oil and cook rapidly, stirring constantly.
• Chop the fennel salami into small pieces. Cook while stirring for 4 minutes. Add the lemon pepper and salt, and let cool.
• Cut the mozzarella into small cubes, let it drain in a colander, and mix well into the cooled filling.
• Divide the dough into four equal pieces and roll out on a floured work surface into thin circles (8" or 20cm diameter). Spoon a quarter of the filling onto one side of the dough circles, but leave the edge free; brush with a little water. Fold the other side of the dough over the filling, press the edges together firmly, and crimp together using the tines of a fork. Prick the top surface several times and sprinkle with Parmesan.
• Put the calzone on a baking sheet lined with baking parchment. Bake on the bottom rack of a preheated oven at 480°F (250°C) for 15 minutes. Serve with a mixed salad.

Spinach Salad with Bacon and Smoked Eggs

Four Servings
2 ounces (50g) of bacon
1 lb. (500-600g) spinach
1 bunch of chives
6 freshly smoked eggs (see page 59)
6 tbsp olive oil
2 tbsp white wine vinegar
4 tsp dijon mustard
Coarse sea salt
Black pepper

• Cut the bacon into thin strips and render the fat in an uncoated pan. Pour off the fat and let the bacon cool.
• Sort the spinach, wash, and drain well.
• Wash the chives, pat dry, and cut into small rolls.
• Peel the eggs and cut into quarters.
• Heat the olive oil in a pan and cookthe onions until translucent; remove from heat and let cool slightly. Mix mustard and vinegar and whisk with the olive oil into a vinaigrette.
• Put the spinach in a large bowl and pour over the vinaigrette. Mix with the bacon and arrange the quartered eggs on top.

Smoked Egg Salad

Four Servings
2 stalks celery
1 bunch of parsley
4 freshly smoked eggs (see page 59)
4 tbsp mayonnaise
2 tsp dijon mustard
Salt
White pepper
2 tbsp small capers
1 small baguette

• Trim and wash the celery; pat dry and cut into small pieces.
• Wash the parsley, pat dry, and chop.
• Halve the eggs and remove the yolk. Mix with the mayonnaise and mustard; add salt and pepper to taste.
• Slice the baguette into 1" thick (3cm) slices and toast.
• Chop the egg whites into small cubes and add with the capers to the mayonnaise mixture. Fold in the celery and capers and serve on the toasted baguette slices.

Appendix

Appendix

Basic Recipes from A to Z

116

Recipes from A to Z

Appendix

Subject Index from A to Z

Common Conversions Used in this Book

This book was originally published in German, and followed the European custom of measuring by metric weight. We have kept the original metric measurements for reference and for those who prefer the precision that can be achieved by cooking by weight.

For those who prefer to cook by measurement using the common U.S. measures, we have made the conversions. For various ingredients measure by weight, we have consulted various conversion calculators to arrive at a volume equivalency.

For liquid measures, we have used the following approximations, leaving the metric measure in parentheses.

50 milliliters (ml)	1 tsp
15 ml	1 tbsp
30 ml	1/8 cup (1oz)
50-65 ml	1/4 cup (2oz)
70-110 ml	1/3 cup
115-130 ml	1/2 cup
135-165 ml	2/3 cup
170-200 ml	3/4 cup
225-250 ml	1 cup
350 ml	1-1/2 cups
400 ml	1-2/3 cups
450-500	2 cups

Glossary

Aging: A process in which cold smoked products are hung for days and sometimes weeks in a cool, airy place; the food "relaxes" or "tenderizes" during this time. As liquids evaporate, the salt and smoke flavors are distributed evenly in the smoked food.

Amino Acids: Building blocks of proteins essential for metabolism and growth processes of the human and animal organism. Many amino acids are made by the body itself; others must be supplied by nourishment.

Antibacterial Effect: Prevents the development or growth of bacteria (single-celled microorganisms).

Antimicrobial Effect: Prevents the development and reproduction of microbes (all microorganisms, including bacteria, fungi, and viruses).

Brining or Pickling: Treating foods — primarily meat — to improve the taste and for preservation. We distinguish between wet curing (salt or vinegar brines) and dry (salt-herb or salt-spice mixtures).

Curing or Pickling: Treating meat with a nitrite pickling salt (NPS). This makes it keep longer, since the nitride has a bactericidal effect (see Antibacterial); it also gives the meat a "reddening" (see Reddening), which preserves the appetizing red color and gives the meat its typical brined flavor.

Drying: After salting or curing, the meat is rinsed and then dried for several hours. For curing, this process is called "infusion" in the jargon and may take several days. It distributes the curing salt throughout the entire piece of meat.

Heaping up the smoking fuel: "Cold smoking" has two steps or phases: smoking and fresh air. For smoking, wood shavings or sawdust are heaped up and lit in the pan or chamber of the smoker; the smoldering fuel produces smoke and starts the smoking process. This is called re-stocking, or heaping up your smoking fuel, and is repeated several times during the smoking process. When you are ready to smoke the meat, you need to pile on some more wood shavings or sawdust on your fire, which will start smoldering to make smoke. Once it stops smoking, you may want to heap up your fire several times, till you get the smoked flavor you want.

Marinating: Treating food to improve the taste. The usual marinade is made with added herbs. Sugar, spices, honey, etc., and alcoholic beverages are also often added.

Nitrate: A chemical compound of nitrogen and oxygen that occurs in the soil. Nitrate is necessary for plant development; it is often used in agriculture as fertilizer. When some vegetables (such as chard, spinach, or beets) are heated repeatedly, nitrate may be transformed into nitrite, which can be harmful at certain levels.

Nitrite: Toxic chemical compound. Larger amounts of nitrite prevent the blood from transporting the vital oxygen to the cells in the body. It is also an ingredient of pickling salt, and is used to preserve meat. What is most important is its bactericidal effect against the dreaded botulism bacteria.

Nitrite pickling salt: This is cooking salt, to which a small, legally regulated amount of sodium nitrite or potassium nitrite is added: 3-1/2 ounces (100g) nitrite pickling salt consists of 3-1/2 ounces (99.4-100g) of cooking salt; it may contain at most 1/50 ounces (0.6g) of nitrite (at least 1/100oz. or 0.4g). You can buy it ready-mixed; you should not mix it yourself.

Nitrosamines: Compound of nitrite and amino acids. These occur in many foods (beer, cheese, fish, fish products, cured meat products, etc.). There is no question that nitrosamines are dangerous for infants up to 8 months old and can be a carcinogen for people of all ages. Nitrosamines are formed especially in cured or smoked meat products. In the industry, ascorbic acid (vitamin C) is often added to these foods, to inhibit nitrosamine formation. Today, nitrosamine concentrations in food products are very low, since nitrite concentrations have been reduced, especially in meat products. As a result, the health risk is considered low.

Osmosis: Complicated process by which two liquids, separated by a membrane and containing different concentration of a solute, attempt to balance theses concentrations. In brining or pickling, osmosis operates when the brine (liquid with a higher salt concentration) penetrates the cell membranes of water-containing meat cells (areas with lower salt concentration) to balance the different salt concentrations on either side.

Reddening: Another term for curing. By a chemical process, the nitrite in curing salts stabilizes the "reddening" of the red muscle pigment myoglobin. Additives, such as sugars or ascorbate, (the salt of ascorbic acid) facilitate this process. When the meat is later cooked or smoked, it keeps its appetizing red color.

Salting: Treating meat with salt that contains no nitrite. Salting alone does not redden the meat. Salted meat does not keep as long as cured meat.

Smoking Steps or Phases: There are two steps to hot smoking: In the first, the fish is cooked at about 195-250°F (90-120°C); the second is the actual smoking process. Here, the temperature is slowly reduced to about 140°F (60°C), and smoke develops.

Cold smoking also includes two phases: first, the food is smoked at 50-75°F (10-25°C) for many hours (usually 6-12). Next, the food is exposed to fresh air, without any smoke; this takes just as long. These two steps are repeated for days, sometimes for weeks.

Smoldering Fire: Caused by the glow of sawdust lit, for example, by a gas flame. Chemists call this process "incomplete combustion." There is no blaze; the fine wood shavings or sawdust only smolder. The hot smoke that arises cooks the food in the smoker.

Smoldering Smoke: The smoke that arises from smoldering firewood or charcoal, through "incomplete combustion"; the fuel does not burn, but just smolders. The resulting smoke cooks the food in the smoker.

Smoke Food the Right Way

Smoked food:

_____

Smoking technique: ◯   ◯   ◯
                      Hot smoking   Warm smoking   Cold smoking

Smoking time:

_____

Amount of wood:

_____

Type of wood:

_____

Smoking temperature:

_____

Herbs and spices:

_____

Remarks:

_____

_____

_____

_____

_____

Smoke Food the Right Way

Smoked food:

_____

Smoking technique: ◯   ◯   ◯
                        Hot smoking   Warm smoking   Cold smoking

Smoking time:

_____

Amount of wood:

_____

Type of wood:

_____

Smoking temperature:

_____

Herbs and spices:

_____

Remarks:

_____

_____

_____

_____

_____

_____

Be <u>Perfectly</u> Prepared

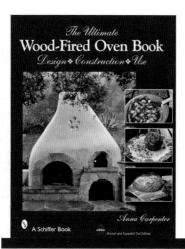